Michael Murphy and Sally Asher

111 Places in New Orleans That You Must Not Miss

111

emons:

© Emons Verlag GmbH
All rights reserved
© Photographs: Sally Asher, except:
p.13, The Abita Mystery House © Derek Hibbs
Painting of Leah Chase on p. 23 reprinted
with permission of the artist, Rise Delmar Ochsner
© Cover icon: shutterstock.com/OZaiachin
Design: Eva Kraskes, based on a design
by Lübbeke | Naumann | Thoben
Edited by Katrina Fried
Maps: altancicek.design, www.altancicek.de
Printing and binding: B.O.S.S Medien GmbH, Goch
Printed in Germany 2015
ISBN 978-3-95451-645-2
First edition

Did you enjoy it? Do you want more?
Join us in uncovering new places around the world on:
www.111places.com

Foreword

New Orleans is as far as you can get from America and still be in it. The historic French and Spanish buildings, plus antebellum homes mixed with shotgun houses, make New Orleans look like nowhere else. Jazz, born in New Orleans, is joined by Cajun, zydeco, brass band, blues, and bounce, making the city sound like no other. Visitors come to the Big Easy on a mission to sample unique Cajun and Creole foods. And New Orleans' history – with plaçage, *coartación*, and Voodoo, plus aboveground burials and cocktails in to-go cups – makes the city seem like a rebellious teenager, willfully trying not to fit in.

Unlike most urban hubs, New Orleans is less about consumption and more about experiences. You need to jump in and participate. There's always a festival or parade happening someplace. Jazz Fest and Essence each draws half a million people. There are three parades every Easter and three vampire balls on Halloween. There are one-of-a-kind events such as Red Dress Run, in which men and women sport red dresses for a mini-marathon sponsored by Hash House Harriers, a "drinking group with a running problem." If you're lucky enough to be in town following another's misfortune, second-line funeral parades have been called New Orleans' quintessential art form. Then, there's the madness of Mardi Gras. During weeks of festivities, classic parades like Zulu and Muses are joined by the Krewe of Barkus, a dog parade, and 'tit Rex, where participants pull tiny doll-house-sized floats strapped to their bicycles.

The following profiles highlight lesser-known spots, favoring the grotto in St. Roch Cemetery over Marie Laveau's grave, and the backyard House of Dance and Feathers museum rather than the World War II Museum. But the truth is that New Orleans is best experienced by wandering around and bumping into things. *111 Places* should not be used as a bucket list, but as a starting point. The goal is to make you an informed flaneur.

111 Places

1 813 Royal Street
The house that saved NOLA

In the heart of the French Quarter, the bungalow-style house at 813 Royal Street barely captures anyone's attention. The address is not mentioned in any guidebook. Yet, it may well be the most important building in New Orleans.

By the 1920s, the Vieux Carré, or French Quarter, was a deteriorated neighborhood which many in the city wished to demolish. Elizabeth Werlein was a transplanted Michigander who enthusiastically embraced the French Quarter, even in its faded splendor. Since moving to New Orleans, she'd been an active society member, a leader in the suffrage movement, an organizer of the Philharmonic Society, and the public relations director of the movie theater chain Saenger.

All of her other accomplishments were to be dwarfed the day she happened to walk by 813 Royal. She saw that a historic building had been torn down and replaced by a California-style house. Appalled, she immediately sprang into action to preserve what remained of the Quarter.

There was already the Vieux Carré Commission (VCC) in 1925, which was an advisory council to protect the neighborhood's history, but it had no teeth and lacked legal power. After years of perseverance, Elizabeth finally convinced the Louisiana Legislature in 1936 to pass a constitutional amendment giving the VCC the authority to block alterations to the centuries-old architecture of the district. In 1939, Elizabeth also bullied the city into granting the commission the power to approve all demolition permits.

She was a one-woman non-wrecking crew, urging property owners to restore their buildings, battling architects when they attempted to replace classic wrought-iron with another material, and inspiring the city's most influential citizens to join the cause to preserve the Vieux Carré. In short, Elizabeth Werlein's activism literally saved the French Quarter – and, in turn, New Orleans – from being just another city.

2 Abita Mystery House

Scratching the itch for kitsch

For most of the most famous roadside attractions, you get to look at whatever the "sight" is – the 10 Cadillacs at Cadillac Ranch outside Amarillo, Lucy the Elephant in New Jersey, or the life-sized statues of the Cabazon Dinosaurs in California – and then you've "done" the thing (note: don't waste your time pulling over to find out what "The Thing" is in Arizona – it's not worth the one buck admission fee). However, once you've entered the Abita Mystery House through a vintage 1930s Standard Oil gas station, your adventure is just beginning.

Located less than an hour's drive from central New Orleans, Abita has a sprawling number of separate buildings, each with its own thematic exhibits of most anything you've imagined in your roadside dreams – or nightmares. You can gaze at the collections of combs and old license plates; play several arcade machines, including one made entirely from popsicle sticks; or use push buttons to animate miniature dioramas of a jazz funeral, a tiny plantation, and a roadside mart called Pinky's What All Store with a little banner that reads "We Got It All."

Out back there's a silver Airstream trailer that was allegedly hit by a flying saucer and a house covered in thousands of fragments of tiles, pottery, mirrors, and glass called the House of Shards. Inside, there's an assortment of weirdness ranging from a vintage bicycle collection to a one-of-a-kind abomination of nature: Bufford the Bassigator, a 22-foot-long half alligator, half fish.

This shrine to tacky taste is the creation of John Preble. The teacher and artist was 50 years old when he finally put a lifetime of odd keepsakes on display for all to see.

Abita Mystery House is also known as the UCM Museum, standing for Unusual Collections and Mini-town, but we suspect Preble intended the name to be pronounced "you-see-em-mu-se-um."

Address 22275 LA-36, Abita Springs, LA 70420, +1 985.892.2624,
www.abitamysteryhouse.com | Hours Daily 10am–5pm | Tip As long as you're out
near Abita Springs, stop off at Abita Beer's Tasting Room for a tour (166 Barbee Rd,
Covington, LA 70433). Established in 1986, Abita Brewing Company is the oldest and
largest craft brewery in the Southeast and one of the oldest in the United States. They are
far and away the most popular local beer, producing more than 150,000 barrels a year.

3__ Aidan Gill for Men

An unapologetically male barbershop

Don't be surprised by the rows of meticulously arranged grooming products and accouterments when you walk into one of Aidan Gill's two barbershops in New Orleans, which are, to quote owner Gill, "unapologetically male." In the 1960s, Dublin native Gill noticed the steady disappearance of barbershops in favor of coed salons and became determined to save the centuries-old trade. He opened his first barbershop in New Orleans in 1990 and is the unequivocal leader of the barbershop resurgence.

His Magazine Street store is a testament to his passion. All of the chairs are vintage Koken or Koch. His mirrors, cabinets, display cases, and bars all have a story (and a purpose). In the back room (the inner sanctum), customers enjoy Gill's signature 30- to 40-minute "Shave at the End of the Galaxy" while sipping some whiskey (or Guinness on tap – your choice), flipping through *Playboys*, admiring Gill's collection of cut-throat razors, all the while being treated to seven steaming towels pulled one by one through the course of a shave from a vintage 1910 steaming machine (no fears, it was retrofitted for electricity).

Gill purchases vintage barbershop memorabilia at auction to display in his shop, saving it from being used as a conversation piece in someone's bathroom. You will also find high-quality items for sale handpicked by Gill himself: tubs of shaving cream, shaving brushes, cowhide razor strops, aftershave, and Gill's own equipment line. What you won't find at Aidan Gill is a female companion hovering by her male, dictating a haircut. Gill has a strict no-female policy and will politely (but firmly) ask them to leave. If they don't comply, the woman and the male customer are shown the door. Gill expertly blends tradition with technology in his shop, but what he doesn't blend is the sexes. "*Unisex* is a dead word in here," Gill states, true to form, very unapologetically.

Address 2026 Magazine Street, New Orleans, LA 70130, +1 504.587.9090, www.aidangillformen.com | Hours Mon–Wed and Fri–Sat 10am–6pm, Thu 10am–7pm, Sun noon–6pm | Tip Ladies, why not pamper yourself while your man is at Aidan Gill? Stroll a couple doors down to Trashy Diva (2048 Magazine St), a local high-end vintage-inspired clothing boutique (and line), which has a cultlike following.

4 Algiers Point

Over da river

There's a ferry at the base of Canal Street, near the aquarium, that crosses the Mississippi River to Algiers Point. It runs every half hour from 6am to 9:45pm during the week, and from 10:45am to 5pm on weekends. Until recently, it was free, but now it'll run you $2 each way. The pleasant, breezy ride is a short five minutes. When visitors ask what there is to do at Algiers Point, the joking response is, "Turn around and come back."

In fact, there are actually several good restaurants and pubs on the point as well as a ton of history and charm. Algiers is the second-oldest neighborhood in New Orleans, after the French Quarter. Slaves, arriving from Africa, used to be held there until they were parceled out. Algiers was also once the hub of slaughterhouses for the city. The first ferry was established in 1823, and by the early 1900s, there were six boats shuttling back and forth, one large enough to carry railroad cars and livestock.

During this time, Algiers also developed a dynamic music scene, with 36 performance venues and dance halls operating by 1911. Many of the top musicians who played the then "newfangled" jazz lived there, including Henry "Red" Allen, Oscar "Papa" Celestine, and Elizabeth "Memphis Minnie" Douglas. New Orleans residents and visitors flowed across the Mississippi to hear live music. Spending an evening there was commonly referred to as going "over da river."

The vast majority of the jazz joints in Algiers have long since disappeared. Most of the saloons are all but forgotten. A "Jazz Walk of Fame," designed with individual honors for 16 pioneering musicians, such as Buddy Bolden and Jelly Roll Morton, has fallen into disrepair. Their portraits were originally illuminated by streetlamps along the levee, but unfortunately, most are now damaged. Even so, the Jazz Walk offers one of the best views of New Orleans' skyline, especially at sunset.

Address Board the ferry to Algiers Point at One Canal Street, New Orleans, LA 70130, www.nolaferries.com; the Jazz Walk of Fame runs along the levee to your right as you exit the ferry at Algiers Point. | **Hours** Ferry runs every half hour; check website for schedule | **Tip** Old Point Bar in Algiers (545 Patterson Dr) has been featured in countless movies because it personifies Hollywood's idea of a neighborhood bar. The small stage hosts some of the city's better musicians, but the headliner is bartender Patti Pujol. She also seems right out of central casting, with her perpetual cowboy hat and an attitude that perfectly balances the line between sweet and smartass.

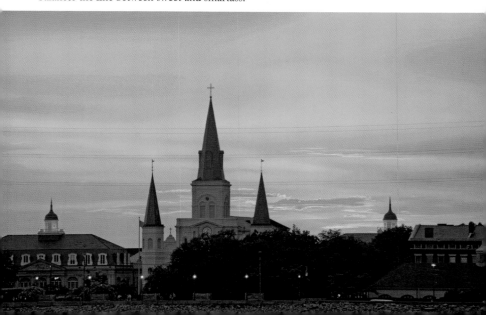

5 Angelo Brocato
Leave the diet, take the cannoli

As a 12-year-old, Angelo Brocato began an apprenticeship in an elegant ice-cream parlor in his hometown of Palermo. After learning the trade, he emigrated from Sicily to the United States and worked on a sugar plantation in New Orleans, trying to save up enough money to open his own shop. In 1905, he opened Angelo's Ice Cream Parlor, a replica of Palermo's finest emporiums, on Ursulines Avenue in the French Quarter. Brocato's moved to Mid-City in 1978, as many residents abandoned the Quarter for outlying neighborhoods.

Today, the shop is run by Angelo Brocato III, and even in its "new" location, remains a throwback to the classic ice-cream parlors of the past. There's an old–world feel created by slowly turning ceiling fans, an archway of lightbulbs over the serving counter, rows of apothecary jars filled with candies, bistro tables, and century-old portraits of Angelo himself on the wall. You are greeted by long glass display cases filled with traditional Italian desserts – handmade zuppa inglese, cassata, Italian fig cookies, spumoni – and New Orleans' best cheesecake. When you order the cannoli, the cone-shaped shell is spoon-filled with a ricotta-cheese-and-sugar mixture right in front of you and dipped in crushed pistachio nuts.

But the main reason to visit Angelo Brocato's is for their 100-year-old Sicilian-recipe gelatos. The flavors filling the display case are all excellent and include two types of pistachio (they are very Sicilian), baci, torroncino, and a great seasonal Louisiana strawberry (much sweeter than traditional strawberry ice cream).

People-watching is another reason to go. On certain nights, the parlor is a mixture of families with kids, heavily pierced and tattooed hipsters, and old Italian men shuffling up to the counter using canes or walkers to order their mini cannoli and double espresso, just as they've been doing for decades.

Address 214 N Carrollton Avenue, New Orleans, LA 70119, +1 504.486.1465, www.angelobrocatoicecream.com | **Hours** Tue–Sun 10am–10pm | **Tip** The original Angelo Brocato's, in the French Quarter (615–617 Ursulines Ave), is now occupied by the coffee and breakfast spot Croissant d'Or Patisserie. You can still see the 100-year-old tiles at the old Brocato's two separate entrances, for "Ladies" and "Gentlemen." Back in the day, men and women used separate doors to avoid the potential scandal of seeing a woman's exposed ankle.

6 Antenna Gallery

A moveable feast of art

The art district in New Orleans shifts like the swampy foundation beneath the city's streets. For many years, the hub was Royal Street and to a lesser extent Chartres Street in the French Quarter. When the Arthur Roger Gallery moved to the Warehouse District in 1988, 12 galleries followed, giving Julia Street the moniker "Gallery Row." For the more intrepid, St. Claude Avenue has become the post-Katrina center for cutting-edge galleries and unconventional artist-run spaces, collectively called SCAD (St. Claude Arts District). (One of the galleries – Barrister's – claims to feature artists "so far removed from the mainstream that the term 'outsider artist' doesn't even begin to describe their current location in space and time.")

Among the gems of St. Claude, and leading the list for art lovers on the hunt for more than a painting that will match their living-room sofa, is the Antenna Gallery, founded by Press Street, a nonprofit dedicated to stimulating art and literature in NOLA. Its two-story building is used, in their words, to produce "an array of risk-taking solo and group exhibitions that engage and interact with the New Orleans community."

Since 2008, Antenna has hosted a variety of never-boring exhibitions, like *My Mom Says My Work Has Really Improved*, a group show that presented the artists' childhood works next to their current works, and *monu_MENTAL*, in which the artists made imaginative revisions to existing local monuments. Another solo exhibition displayed a series of machines that had been repurposed into art-making gadgets, like a weed cutter rigged to draw grass, and a car with a retrofitted engine that was made to sketch a rudimentary self-portrait when visitors sat inside and turned the steering wheel.

A great time to do a gallery crawl through SCAD is on the second Saturday night of the month, when many venues hold openings for new exhibitions.

Address 3718 St. Claude Street, New Orleans, LA 70117, +1 504.298.3161,
www.press-street.org | Hours Tue–Sun noon–5pm | Tip If you happen to be in
New Orleans around Thanksgiving, each year Press Street produces the Draw-a-thon, a free
24-hour drawing extravaganza where more than 700 artists and non-artists of all ages make
art based on a theme, often in inventive ways, like tracing shadows on walls. Press Street
describes the event as "creating for the sake of creating, process over product."

7__ The Art of Dooky Chase

These walls can talk

Dooky Chase's Restaurant has been a revered New Orleans' institution since 1941. Ms. Leah Chase married into the family that owned the restaurant and started working there in 1957. She thought she was being hired to be the hostess, but wound up back in the kitchen. A self-taught chef, Chase went on to win every culinary award imaginable. Known as the outspoken Queen of Creole Cuisine, she once chastised President Obama when he started to put hot sauce in her gumbo, giving him a double dose of "Oh no you don't!" for even thinking of messing with her perfect recipe.

As delicious as her gumbo and fried chicken are (the latter was recently voted the best in New Orleans), the art on the restaurant's walls may be the most memorable thing you'll savor. Ms. Chase received her first painting, a work by the artist Jacob Lawrence, as a present from her husband. Over the next 50 years, she assembled a remarkable collection of art by African Americans; some pieces were gifts, some were traded for meals, and others were acquired from the artists. Ms. Chase received a first-class education in art from Celestine Cook, a civic leader and the first African American to sit on the board of the New Orleans Museum of Art.

Highlights of the collection include works by Elizabeth Catlett, John Biggers, and a series of portraits of Ms. Chase by Gustave Blache III. While she sat for Blache, she implored, "I hope you're making me look like Halle Berry." Two of Blache's paintings depicting Chase at work now hang in the Smithsonian National Portrait Gallery.

When the levees broke in the wake of Hurricane Katrina, Dooky Chase's was terribly flooded. Thankfully, one of Ms. Chase's grandsons was able to remove all the art before any damage was done. Today, visitors can dine on Ms. Chase's award-winning cuisine in what remains one of the finest African-American art galleries in the city – perhaps in the country.

Address 2301 Orleans Avenue, New Orleans, LA 70119, +1 504.821.0600,
www.dookychaserestaurant.com | Hours Tue–Fri 11am–3pm (lunch); Fri 5pm–9pm
(dinner) | Tip There's no shortage of places for great fried chicken in New Orleans.
Others high on anyone's list would be the James Beard Award-winning Willie
Mae's Scotch House (2401 St. Ann St); Fiorella's (1136 Decatur St); McHardy's
(1458 N Broad St); and Manchu Food Store (1413 N Claiborne St), where you
pay for takeout through bulletproof glass.

8__ Audubon Park Labyrinth
Walking a sacred path

There are many reasons to go to Audubon Park. You can exercise by walking, running, or biking the 1.8-mile trail, which takes you by a sculpture garden and Ochsner Island, a rookery that attracts hundreds of bird species. The path also encircles the Audubon golf course, originally built in 1898, then renovated in 2002. A huge rock sits in the middle of the 18th fairway. There are conflicting stories about the origins of the 15-ton, 8-foot-high boulder; some say it's a meteor that struck the earth in 1891, while others maintain it's merely an abandoned chunk of iron ore that was on display at the Alabama State exhibit in the Cotton Centennial in 1884.

The newest reason to go is a walking labyrinth, unveiled on Easter Sunday 2006. Its creator, stone sculptor Marty Kermeen, duplicated the specific measurements used in archetypal labyrinths all over the world. Labyrinths have an unknown origin but are recorded in many ancient civilizations. The most famous is in the floor of the Cathedral at Chartres, about an hour outside Paris. It was completed in A.D. 1220.

The labyrinth's symbol of the spiral is the universal representation of transformation. Unlike mazes, labyrinths are not intended to challenge or confuse with blind alleys and dead ends; they offer just one path to the center. By traversing the twists and turns and making one's way to the middle, the mind is opened to receive the spirit.

Over the last decade or so, the labyrinth as a meditation tool has had a resurgence. There are modern labyrinth societies. There's even an annual World Labyrinth Day, on May 2. Grace Cathedral in San Francisco has a labyrinth on the chapel floor and another outdoors, plus they sell seed kits to make the same design and proportions anywhere.

The labyrinth in Audubon Park not only can open your mind, but also can help walk off all those beignets and bread puddings from your waistline.

Address Audubon Park, midway between the St. Charles and Magazine Streets side entrances, near East Drive, where Laurel Street dead ends into the park | Hours Daily 5am – 10pm | Tip Audubon Park contains plenty of treasured spots, including the city's zoo, home of 2000 animals, jokingly said to have a recipe card in front of each because Louisiana folk will eat anything and everything. The Fly is also a lovely area right on the Mississippi River, with baseball and soccer fields and plenty of space to lounge or picnic. The Cascade Stables has 40 privately owned and boarded horses, but also provides horseback lessons to visitors.

9__ Bacchanal
Just like it sounds (plus tiki torches)

Friday lunch at Galatoire's is one kind of signature dining event in New Orleans. A dozen oysters at Casamento's and breakfast at Brennan's are others. In the aftermath of Hurricane Katrina, a Sunday-night meal at Bacchanal joined their ranks.

Chris Rudge had opened Bacchanal in Bywater in 2002 as an unassuming corner wine shop, a stone's throw from the Industrial Canal and the Mississippi River. This was "pre-gentrification," when Bywater was still considered a sketchy neighborhood. Rudge started hosting casual once-a-week dinners in the garden patio behind his 200-year-old building, where he provided renowned guest chefs like Peter Vazquez and Dan Esses the opportunity to keep their mojo alive after the storm while their former restaurants were being repaired or relocated. The backyard party became so popular with locals, Bacchanal eventually hired a full-time chef, Joaquin Rodas, and expanded their meals to seven days a week. Rodas was born in El Salvador, grew up in Los Angeles, and moved to New Orleans in 1995. Much of his menu consists of delicious and inventive small plates. Perhaps the best single bite in the city is one of Rodas' bacon-wrapped dates with chorizo, pequillo peppers, and roasted tomatoes.

What raises Bacchanal from a great meal to a great experience is the live music and almost magical environment. Seated outdoors under strings of tiny lights and surrounded by tiki torches, you're entertained by noted New Orleans musicians. Onstage every Monday night is Helen Gillet – hailed by *DownBeat* magazine as "one of the best musicians in town – and that's saying a lot." On Thursdays, the Courtyard Kings perform a mash-up of bebop, gypsy jazz, and Brazilian and New Orleans jazz.

Rudge died in 2015 at the far-too-young age of 40, but not before he saw his ever-morphing vision become a distinctive – some might say essential – New Orleans experience.

Address 600 Poland Avenue, New Orleans, LA 70117, +1 504.948.9111, www.bacchanalwine.com | **Hours** Daily 11am – midnight; no reservations (there's usually a line on weekends) | **Tip** In the past few years, Bywater has evolved from blue collar to dangerously close to hipster. There has been an accompanying surge of new premier restaurants. Those receiving the highest praise include Maurepas Foods, Oxalis, Mariza, and Booty's Street Food.

10___The Batture
Waterfront (sometimes water-infused) property

If you ask ten locals how to get to the batture, nine are likely not to know what you're talking about. The tenth might reply, "Why do you want to go *there*?"

The word *batture* refers to the entire strip of land that runs between a levee and river. Once entirely populated, New Orleans' batture was a part of the city almost since the beginning, but now it is down to only about a dozen quirky residences that are built on pilings and stamped into the edge of the Mississippi River. Once characterized as truly fringe, these days you'll find this little-known area is becoming more of a mixed community, where newly constructed or renovated homes stand alongside the original ramshackle houses known as "camps."

Separated from the rest of New Orleans by the levee wall, the batture still feels like a world unto itself, and much of its eccentricity remains. In 2011, NPR did a story in which they interviewed some of its residents. One, Jean Brady Hendricks, used to be a performer in the burlesque clubs on Bourbon Street. Around the time the classic venues were replaced by much raunchier joints, Jean, then in her mid-eighties, moved out to the batture to live in isolated peace. Macon Fry, another resident, is an urban farmer and educator. He built the house he lives in from salvaged wood. Macon can also wax poetic about his chosen community. He described his homestead this way: "It's not in the city, and it's not really in the river. But it's on the edge, and there's a lot of interesting things that happen on edges."

The people who live on the batture surely cherish their otherness and solitude. No doubt they don't want the "neighborhood" to be soiled by tourists. But you can still respectfully wander the community and see folk sculptures created out of whatever's washed ashore – or just watch as the river flows up into people's yards and underneath their homes.

Address Located on the Mississippi River, roughly between Dakin Street and Monticello Avenue where they intersect with River Road, at the Jefferson-Orleans parish line. | Tip After a walk on the wild side, you will be close to a cluster of noteworthy restaurants at what's called the Riverbend, or where St. Charles Ave turns a corner to become Carrollton. You can eat at New Orleans' most famous burger joint, Camellia Grill (626 S Carrollton Ave), or Cooter Brown's (509 S Carrollton Ave), a sports bar with 21 TVs and 400 brands of beer, or go upscale and dine at the James Beard Award-winning Brigsten's (723 Dante St).

11_ The Bead Tree

Beads for needs

Mardi Gras in New Orleans is believed to have started in the 1830s. The first "throws" were introduced in 1872, when sugarcoated almonds were tossed to onlookers by the king of the Krewe of Rex. Throws date back to a custom from Renaissance England. As the popularity of the parades grew toward the end of the 19th century, bringing over 100,000 visitors each season, strings of glass beads became the popular throw. Locals collected them. Visitors took them home as souvenirs. Cheaper to produce and less dangerous to onlookers, plastic beads replaced glass beads in the 1960s.

Like Easter bonnets and Santa hats, Mardi Gras beads should only be worn in season, unless you want to make absolutely clear you are a tourist or conventioneer. Beads, however, can be seen in our trees year round. The trees along St. Charles Avenue, the main parade route, look like a children's storybook brought to life just after the Mardi Gras season. Errant throws from krewe members on the floats get stuck in the branches and glimmer in gold, red, blue, purple, silver, pink, and green.

There is one tree behind Gibson Hall on the Tulane campus where the beads are not accidental. To mark the beginning of each new Mardi Gras season, university students, with purpose and resolve, toss shiny new strands onto an oak tree on the academic quad, turning the tree into a colorful monument.

In 2013, Tulane hosted a post-Mardi Gras festivity called the Bead Tree Bonanza. Students and others took the mountains of beads collected during the parades and donated them to Arc Enterprises, a nonprofit that provides employment opportunities to people with developmental disabilities. Participants in Arc are hired every year to sift through and separate the donated beads for reuse the next year. Used beads can be dropped off at the Arc Recycling Center (www.arcgno.org/arc-enterprises).

Address Behind Gibson Hall (between West and Law Roads, off St. Charles Avenue) on Tulane's campus | Tip In addition to beads, other Mardi Gras throws include Frisbees, glow-in-the-dark pins, rings, necklaces, balls, plastic swords, mini footballs, fake flowers, plush toys, lace underwear – pretty much anything. The most coveted throws are decorated coconuts, given out by the Zulu krewe, and the highly glittered and glamorized shoes of the Krewe of Muses.

12 Bottom of the Cup

Top-of-the-heap psychic readings

Since opening in 1929, Bottom of the Cup has enjoyed a reputation for being not just the most venerable place for psychic readings in New Orleans, but also the most accurate and authentic. (You can get a less-expensive reading a few blocks away on Jackson Square – but be warned, you'll get what you pay for.) Bottom of the Cup started out as a tearoom where shoppers in the midst of walking and eating their way through the French Quarter could relax. After they finished their cup of Earl Grey or chamomile, a fortune-teller would come by the table and read the remaining leaves. The shop still serves tea – they offer more than 100 types, from the familiar to the rare – and also sells a wide variety of metaphysical gift items like hanging charms, crystal balls, pendulums, and tarot card decks; but they remain best known for their psychics.

While all their readers are noteworthy, some have achieved celebrity status. Former owner Adele Mullen, who passed away in 2007, was one of the more famous. She left her career as a teacher to join the family business and discovered that her gifts for predicting the future exceeded her talents for correcting grammar. During her stewardship of the shop, national TV and radio networks sought her out for annual Superbowl predictions.

Today's star is Otis Biggs. He's been divining the future at Bottom of the Cup since 1972. Otis is a versatile psychic, reading tea leaves, cards, and palms, or using only his natural clairvoyant abilities without the aid of any tools at all. His prophecies – from serious economic forecasts to major sports outcomes – have been featured in numerous print and media outlets.

Bottom of the Cup provides an audio recording of your session so you can refresh your memory on the mantras you were supposed to repeat or go back to check the veracity of the predictions made whenever you like.

Address 327 Chartres Street, New Orleans, LA 70130, +1 800.729.7148, www.bottomofthecup.com | Hours Daily 10am–6pm | Tip If you're looking for traditional high tea without a reading, there are three elegant spots: La Salon in the Windsor Court Hotel (300 Gravier St), the Davenport Lounge at the Ritz Carlton (921 Canal St), and the Victorian-style Albertine's Tea Room in the Columns Hotel (3811 St. Charles St).

13 Bourbon Orleans Hotel
Dancing with the dead

Opened in 1817, the Bourbon Orleans Hotel has a rich – and somewhat bizarre – history. It was originally built as the Orleans Ballroom by entrepreneur John Davis, who also built the adjacent opera house. Both buildings were later used as a convent for girls.

But the hotel was most famously the setting for quadroon balls, where wealthy white gentlemen would meet mixed-race young women to take them on as well cared for mistresses in a practice known as *plaçage*. These women would be educated, often in Europe, and then housed in cottages in what is now the Marigny neighborhood. Their male benefactors would live with them part of the year and with their wives back in the French Quarter the rest of the time. *Plaçage* was an aboveboard and accepted tradition. You have to wonder if the wives didn't look forward to those periods when their husbands, with their stinky cigars and randomly tossed socks, would be out of the house.

The Bourbon Orleans is considered haunted by a number of spirits. Some guests have reported being slapped on the wrists after swearing, presumably by the ghost of a nun from the convent days. There have been sightings of a soldier in a dark uniform from either the Civil War or the War of 1812. His name is Eldridge. There are "ladies of the evening," one seen in lightning-fast glimpses dancing across the courtyard. Most famous is the Lady in Red, who has frequently been seen dancing alone in the ballroom on the second floor.

There are two things worth noting in the first-floor lobby. First is the double-sided stairway leading to the ballroom. Back in the day, it was scandalous for a gentleman to see the ankle of a young woman. Therefore, men and women took separate staircases. Second, to the left of the check-in desk is a display case showing historic artifacts. One is an old vampire kit, with crucifix, stake, garlic, et al. Families used to keep vampire kits handy, much as today they might keep Band-Aids and peroxide in the cabinet.

Address 717 Orleans Street, New Orleans, LA 70112, +1 504.523.2222, www.bourbonorleans.com | **Tip** One of the scarier though equally beautiful sights in New Orleans at night is just to the left upon exiting the Bourbon Orleans Hotel. Lit from beneath, the statue of Jesus in the courtyard behind the St. Louis Cathedral casts a long shadow against the church that looks more like the Son of Dracula than the Son of God.

14 Boutique du Vampyre
One-stop shopping for all your vampire needs

If you are into vampires, or really think you are a vampire, you've come to the right city. New Orleans has a long history of vampires and openly embraces this most alternative of alternative lifestyles. There is a vampire bar, the Dungeon (738 Toulouse Street), where the dance floor is a mirror, which presumably does not reflect a number of the patrons. NOVA (The New Orleans Vampire Association) is a nonprofit association dedicated to the support and promotion for people who identify themselves as vampires. At Halloween each year, there are three vampire balls. The city even hosts a vampire convention, the Undead Con, featuring vampire novelists and artisans.

And then there is the Boutique du Vampyre – the only brick-and-mortar vampire shop in America, and one of just three in the world. Marita Jaeger, who cheekily claims to be a vampire herself, created and runs the store. She is another in a long line of visitors who was seduced by New Orleans and never left. Her shop is filled with handmade treasures crafted by 130 local artisans. Maven Lore, a renowned local fangsmith (one who makes fangs), will even meet you at the shop by appointment and make you a custom set of fangs, color matched to your teeth – the prices range from $100 to $800.

Here you can buy candles; pewter charms; vampire perfume by Hove, a 100-year-old perfumer on Chartres Street; hot sauce made in Transylvania, Louisiana; museum-quality shrunken heads from Ecuador; steampunk skulls; and the ever-popular vampire lesson box, which includes a welcome letter, votive candle, sealing wax, and instructions and advice from centuries-old vampires. The shop also sells temporary bite-mark tattoos, emergency stake wall units (just break glass), and vampire spirits that have been trapped and sealed in bottles. In other words, pretty much everything an actual or aspiring vampire might want to consume, from A positive to O.

Address 709 1/2 St. Ann Street, New Orleans, LA 70116, +1 504.561.8267, www.feelthebite.com | Hours Daily 10am–9pm | Tip Clinton, LA, the setting for the fictional town of Bon Temps on HBO's vampire series *True Blood*, is just an hour and forty-five minutes' drive from New Orleans. The show employed more than 50 local residents as characters and extras. Years ago, Clinton was also the setting for the popular series *The Dukes of Hazzard*.

15 Casa Borrega

A feast for the senses

Billed as an authentic Mexican restaurant, Casa Borrega is also a hotbed for South-American and Mexican music, and every bit as much an art installation as it is a terrific place to eat. At the center of it all is Hugo Montero, a gregarious artist who moved to New Orleans from Mexico City. The co-star is his wife, Linda Stone, an environmentalist whose passion for recycling and re-use, paired with Hugo's artistic flair, has resulted in the transformation of a 19th-century house into the most visually arresting restaurant in this and most any other city.

You could spend the first half of the meal surveying the myriad decorative touches, letting your tostadas and panuchos get cold. Everything in the interior is salvaged and repurposed. The tables are all handmade, as is the stained glass in the windows. Iron chandeliers from Mexico hang from the ceiling and vintage guitars line the walls leading to the restrooms. The ceiling fans are stunning artifacts Hugo acquired from an old hotel in Cuba. Above the bar, there's a two-headed demon-boy piñata riding in an antique children's car. Ceramic skulls are everywhere inside; little altars are everywhere outside on the patio. Some nights, the restaurant hosts bands on a small stage that's equally covered in eccentric objects.

The food is "real" Mexican, unlike what you may be used to. Hugo states, "I adore Tex-Mex, but it's not Mexican." They don't serve burritos or cheesy gordita crunch. Casa Borrega's menu has traditional dishes like the must-order Coctel de Camarones, a shrimp cocktail appetizer served in a large margarita glass, and entrees like the Borrega: slow-braised lamb cooked in tequila and mescal. Side bowls made from hollowed-out gourds are filled with black beans and guacamole.

Hugo and Linda call their restaurant a *peña*. *Peña* is a Mexican word for a community meeting place where food and drink share equal billing with artistic expression.

Address 1719 Oretha Castle Haley Boulevard, New Orleans, LA 70113, +1 504.427.0654, www.casaborrega.com | **Hours** Tue–Thu 11:30am–2:30pm (lunch) 5pm–9:30pm (dinner), Fri and Sat 11:30am–10:30pm | **Tip** You can also get authentic El Salvador food at La Macarena (8120 Hampson St). There's a good chance you may wonder if you want authentic Salvadoran food because you don't know what it is. Their main dish is the pupusa, a flat masa-dough disk filled with sour cheese, beans, and usually, bits of pork. Think of them as stuffed Mayan pancakes. If you're still lost, the affable owner, Manny Ochoa-Galvez, will be only too happy to serve as your guide.

16_Chainsaw Tree

An old oak's rebirth

The majestic oak trees on Bayou St. John in Mid-City offer shade for picnickers, casual fishermen, musicians, and those who come to watch the Mardi Gras Indians dance and strut along the bayou on Super Sunday. Hurricane Katrina took out some of the oaks but the one that was closest the Orleans Avenue Bridge near the south end of the bayou managed to survive – only to be killed by lightning during Hurricane Isaac in 2012.

Bayou Boogaloo, a free local music and art festival held on the bayou every May, decided to try and give the tree new life. Enter sculptor Marlin Miller, a chainsaw artist from Florida who sells wooden sculptures in galleries across the country. His work ranges in size (and price) from small to large (and from hundreds to thousands of dollars). Miller's true passion, however, is creating carvings from dead trees, resurrecting them as pieces of art. After witnessing Hurricane Katrina's devastation, Miller carved animals indigenous to the Gulf Coast into trees along U.S. 90 through Biloxi and Gulfport, Mississippi. Bayou Boogaloo contacted Miller, whose chainsaw company pays for his expenses, but who donates his time for free, to see if he could do something with the oak on the bayou. Miller receives constant requests but has strict criteria for a tree: it must be a large oak or a hardwood, on public property in a visible area, and – most important – it must have emotion. Fortunately, the semi-charred tree on the bayou checked all those boxes.

In May 2013, Miller (battling against sometimes uncooperative weather) carved symbols and icons of New Orleans into the hardy trunk and branches still standing: a large pelican, various fish and birds, musical instruments, a prominent fleur de lis, and a Mardi Gras Indian who keeps a watchful eye on the street traffic on the bridge. The Chainsaw Tree may no longer offer shade, but it still offers a great view.

Address On the lakeside bank of Bayou St. John, adjacent to the Orleans Avenue Bridge |
Tip Walk over to NOLA Til Ya Die (3536 Toulouse St), a local clothing and accessories
company founded after Katrina to represent locals' commitment to New Orleans. Pick up
a shirt, sticker, flask, or flag to show your commitment to the Big Easy.

17 __ Checkpoint Charlie's

Come for the band, leave with clean socks

If you're in need of a standard, harshly lit, 24-hour laundromat with a battery of huge front-loading dryers that will require a paycheck's worth of quarters to make it through two loads, Checkpoint Charlie's is not your spot. Yes, they have washing machines, but that's the least of their selling points. Standing on a corner of Esplanade Avenue, alongside the French Quarter and at the mouth of Frenchmen Street, New Orleans music alley, Checkpoint Charlie's is a bar, a game room, a live music venue, and a laundromat, all rolled into one. (The actual name is *Igor's* Checkpoint Charlie, but no one calls it that.)

Waiting for your socks and sweaters to dry, there's much more to do here than read year-old magazines. The small stage delivers – depending on the night – a mix of rock, metal and punk, and some performers who aren't welcome anywhere else. Regular bands include Bible Belt Sinners, Bad Moon Lander, and the Olivia de Havilland Mosquitoes. Tuesday evenings offer a popular weekly open-mic blues jam. There's a pool table, a pinball machine, and arcade games aplenty. If you dare, you can also order their half-pound Charlie Burger, jalapeno poppers, mini-pizzas, chicken nuggets, tater tots, or cheese fries.

This is a dive that seems to relish its dive-iness. The drinks are cheap. The staff members have an edge but are, by and large, friendly and gracious. The bathrooms, however, come with a warning: don't use them. As an online reviewer wrote, they "would be considered a disgrace in most third world countries."

Anything can and often does happen inside Checkpoint Charlie's. One night a bongo-playing stranger joined famed guitarist Jimmy Robinson onstage and played the entire night. Occasionally a fight might break out, but they remain isolated and cause very little damage or ruckus, so you can keep nursing your drink and wait out the spin cycle.

Address 501 Esplanade Avenue, New Orleans, LA 70116, +1 504.281.4847 | **Hours** Open 24 hours | **Tip** While skirmishes at Checkpoint Charlie's are few and inconsequential, a fight between rival biker gangs in a French-Quarter tattoo parlor fundamentally changed the neighborhood. Residents pushed through an ordinance banning tattoo parlors from the Vieux Carré. You will now find them stacked up on the immediate outskirts.

18 City Park's Live Oaks
A family of trees

There are majestic and iconic live oak trees accented with Spanish moss and resurrection fern throughout the American South, but City Park is home to one of the largest and oldest live oak forests in the world. The park lost roughly 2000 trees following Hurricane Katrina because they stood in five feet of brackish water for weeks. Otherwise, the live oak is nearly impervious to hurricane-force winds because the massive trunk and expansive limbs you see above ground are mirrored by an extraordinary root system. There remain 20,000 trees in the 1,300-acre park. Most of the live oaks predate the founding of New Orleans 300 years ago.

The unusual aspect about the City Park trees is that so many have been given personal names and identities. The massive McDonogh Oak is named after the shipping magnate and philanthropist who donated land to form City Park. It has a circumference of 25 feet and is about 800 years old. The Singing Oak was designed by Jim Hart as a post-Katrina tribute to rebuilding the city. Seven wind chimes hang on the tree. The chimes are tuned to the pentatonic scale, used by West-African music, early gospel, and jazz, all of which represent the roots of New Orleans music. The Suicide Oak is so called because in the span of 12 years, 16 men committed suicide under its branches for reasons of broken hearts or busted bank accounts.

The best known and most visited is the remaining one of two Dueling Oaks, which stands just southwest of the art museum. Before they were outlawed in the late 1800s, countless duels took place under the two trees, using pistols, knives, and particularly swords. Disagreements about the merits of an opera or a gentleman moving his chair too close to another man's date could result in a duel. A European visitor got bloodied in a duel after he insulted the Mississippi River by calling it "but a tiny rill compared to the great rivers of Europe."

Address City Park, One Palm Drive, New Orleans, LA 70124, 1+ 504.482.4888; a map of the live oaks in City Park can be found at: www.neworleanscitypark.com/in-the-park/city-park-map | **Tip** City Park is also home to the New Orleans Museum of Art and Sculpture Garden; the New Orleans Botanical Garden; City Putt, the only miniature golf course in the city; Morning Call, a 24-hour beignet coffee stand; Storyland, a kiddie theme park with 25 fiberglass sculptures to climb; and one of the oldest carousels in the United States, which locals call the "flying horses." Some of the carved horses date back to 1885.

19__Claiborne Corridor

Historic past with a possible future

Claiborne Avenue is one of longest and most storied streets in the city. Running through Tremé, the section from Orleans Avenue to Elysian Fields was once a thriving commercial district for African Americans, who were long denied access to the whites-only shops and movie palaces on Canal Street and much of the French Quarter.

At the time, Claiborne had a wide neutral ground (the New Orleans term for a median) lined four deep with live oaks, almost like a park in the middle of the street, where area residents would congregate. Slowly, under the guise of modernization, the neighborhood was torn apart. The final death knell came in the 1960s with the white flight to suburbia and the development of a highway system to serve these outlying communities. Five hundred homes were torn down to facilitate construction of a new interstate. The green median along Claiborne Avenue was ripped up and replaced by concrete. Not surprisingly, the business district rapidly declined as the community's center disintegrated.

Today, this stretch of Claiborne is a ramshackle mix of vacant homes, used tire shops, and convenience stores, all under the shadow of the freeway that passes overhead. There is, however, a glimmer of hope to be found in the Restore the Oaks program. In 2002 the African American Museum issued a call to local artists to create a permanent outdoor exhibit using the large cement pillars that hold up the highway as their canvases. Many paintings depict the grand trees that used to stand there. Others memorialize the people of historic Tremé and the Seventh Ward, like gospel singer Mahalia Jackson, musician Fats Domino, and inventor Norbert Rillieux.

In the wake of Hurricane Katrina, there's been a more fervent call to rethink the I-10 and explore the possibility of removing the entire 2.2-mile elevated stretch of highway to free up more than 50 acres of land and restore the vibrancy of the area.

Address North Claiborne Avenue from Elysian Fields to Orleans Avenue, New Orleans, LA 70116 | **Tip** All medians in New Orleans are called neutral grounds. This comes from Canal St, the dividing line between the European residents in the French Quarter and the Americans on the Uptown side. While thinking each other idiots, the median was the one place they agreed not to squabble.

20__The Cornstalk Hotel

A hotel with apparitional amenities

The charming Cornstalk Hotel was built in the early 1800s as the home of Judge Francois-Xavier Martin, first chief justice of the Louisiana Supreme Court. The hotel's namesake comes from the exterior wrought-iron fence shaped to look like a row of corn. The story goes that the wife of one of the later owners was from Iowa and suffered from homesickness. To help ease her pain, her husband had the fence made to remind her of home. In fact, however, there are two other houses in New Orleans with the exact same railing, and the fence design used to be listed in the ornamental ironwork catalog of Wood & Perot of Philadelphia ... There's a phrase we use in New Orleans (a lot): "Never let the truth get in the way of a good story."

There are chandeliers gracing most of the spacious bedrooms, but the bathrooms are so small you have to leave the room to change your mind. It's particularly enjoyable to sit out on the second-floor balcony with a cigar or a glass of wine and watch the people strolling along Royal Street as the bats flutter overhead.

The Cornstalk has hosted a number of famous guests, including the Clintons and Harriet Beecher Stowe. Fans of the "King" can request the Elvis Room, which is where Presley stayed while he was in town filming *King Creole*.

The Cornstalk is also one of the city's many haunted hotels. Reported paranormal activity includes the sounds of children running and laughing, and light footsteps in the halls when no one is there. But what truly sets the Cornstalk apart are the "polterazzi." There are tales of guests staying alone in a room and waking up the next day to discover photographs of themselves on their cameras or cell phones, apparently taken during the night while they slept. Especially goose bump producing is the added fact that the photos appear to have been taken from ... the ceiling.

Address 915 Royal Street, New Orleans, LA 70116, +1 504.523.1515,
www.thecornstalkhotel.com | Tip Elvis Presley considered *King Creole*, filmed in
New Orleans, his best picture. The movie opens with Elvis singing from a small window
overlooking a flurry of street vendors below. The song, "Crawfish," is a classic, but one
whose lyrics have it all wrong. To catch a crawfish, you don't "put a big long hook on a
big long pole," and you'd never "fry him crisp" – there's only one way to cook crawfish in
New Orleans: you boil 'em, period. Never let the truth get in the way of a good song.

21__Crescent Park

Reinventing the waterfront

Crescent Park, New Orleans' newest public green space, opened in 2015 after nine years of planning, design, and construction. The park, which borders the Mississippi River from Elysian Fields Avenue in the Marigny to Mazant Street in Bywater, successfully transformed 1.4 miles of waterfront – long abandoned by the once bustling shipping industry – without blotting out the character and history of the surroundings.

The city broke ground on the park in late 2010, implementing the designs of at least three architecture firms in a coordinated effort with the U.S. Army Corps of Engineers, Port of New Orleans, New Orleans Public Belt Railroad, the Sewerage and Water Board, Landis Construction, the Tobler Company, and subcontractor Rotolo Consultants. With that many cooks, it's a minor miracle the park ever came to be.

The multi-use urban park includes 20 acres of native landscaping, walking and biking paths lined with crape myrtle and oaks; a pedestrian promenade that runs from end to end; picnic areas, benches, and even a small dog run – all with rediscovered and spectacular views of the city's skyline, Algiers Point, and the Mississippi. The decaying Piety Wharf was partially repaired to be a vista point, and the Mandeville Shed, another abandoned wharf, has been converted into an open-air community and event space. Streets that intersect the park are elegantly marked with stone blocks chiseled with their names.

The most eye-catching feature of the new park is the massive Piety Street Bridge, nicknamed "The Rusty Rainbow." Designed by Tanzanian architect David Adjaye, the steeply pitched, raw and rusty steel archway allows pedestrians to cross over the levee wall and the riverfront railroad tracks to reach the newly sodded gardens. The bridge is quickly becoming an iconic photographer's spot, rivaling St. Louis Cathedral and the St. Charles streetcar.

Address Chartres Street from Elysian Fields Avenue to Mazant Street | **Hours** Daily 8am–6pm | **Tip** East of the park in Bywater is a rocky spit where the Mississippi River meets the Industrial Canal. Locally, it is known as the End of the World Beach. From here one can watch large vessels on the river flow by, but the real beauty of the spot is the meditative sound of water lapping against half-submerged trees. To reach the "beach," walk east past Mazant St on Chartres St for 3 1/2 blocks and take a left on Poland Ave. Walk four blocks and take a right on N Rampart St, which runs into a footpath. Follow the path to its terminus.

22 DBC
Drive-thru daiquiris

You'll need a car to enjoy one of New Orleans' quirkiest local institutions – the Drive-Thru Daiquiri stand. The sazerac may be the official state cocktail and tourists might stumble around the Quarter holding on to hurricanes, but the frozen daiquiri is the everyman's drink of choice in Louisiana. They are a staple at Jazz Fest and in Mardi Gras crowds, at backyard barbecues and movie theaters – the Audubon Zoo even sells them in animal-themed souvenir cups.

Originally of Cuban origin, the daiquiri was introduced to America by David Briggs, when he opened the first New Orleans Original Daiquiris stand in 1983. The slushy drink starts with the basics of rum, lime juice, and sugar, and then launches in a variety of technicolor fruity directions with names like Shockwave, Jagerburn, and one simply called Abuse. They are served in cups sized from small to family size to "The Monster," a gallon-sized portion. Prices run from $5 to $25 depending on the size, and for a slight up-charge, you can order extra shots.

If you wonder how selling alcoholic drinks at drive-thru windows is the least bit legal, here's how it works. As long as the booze is in a sealed cup, the drive-thru is in accordance with the law. Therefore, the wrapped straw is presented separately from the cup. Some daiquiri shops even tape over the straw hole on the lid. Clearly, between the tape barrier and unopened straw, there is no conceivable way a driver can imbibe before getting home.

For whatever reason (they all look pretty much alike), DBC's drive-thru in Metairie has become a hometown favorite. DBC, which stands for Daiquiri Bay Cafe, also has 40 brands of beer, but you go for the daiquiris. If you just can't decide which one to order, they offer the "Kitchen Sink," which is sort of like giving a kid free access to the bank of soda fountains in a fast-food restaurant – it's a scary concoction of all the flavors mixed together.

Address 1001 Veterans Memorial Boulevard, Metairie, LA 70005, +1 504.838.2282, www.dbcbarandgrill.com | Hours Daily, 11am until the last customer leaves | Tip Open Container laws make it possible to drink alcohol in public in Savannah, Georgia, but only in the Historic District and only 16 ounces or less. In Memphis you can just drink on a section of Beale Street, in Las Vegas only on the Strip. In Butte, Montana, you can drink anywhere, but you're in Butte. You can drink anything you want, wherever you want, and any amount you desire throughout New Orleans.

23_Dew Drop Jazz Hall

Worshipping in the house of jazz

Across Lake Pontchartrain, on a tree-lined side street in the town of Mandeville, sits what looks like an old country church. In many ways it is. The spirits of jazz history are alive in its unpainted wood plank walls. Built in 1895, the Dew Drop is the oldest jazz hall in the United States.

A group of civic-minded African Americans created the Dew Drop Social and Benevolent Association to provide for the needy. They built the hall to be their headquarters, but it quickly evolved into a hub for jazz musicians. After playing more traditional music for whites-only audiences throughout the week, New Orleans jazz pioneers began rushing across the lake to cut loose for black audiences. The Dew Drop's alumni represent a virtual who's who of jazz greats, most notably, Louie Armstrong, who played there when he needed a break from the demands of his growing international celebrity.

By the 1940s, an emerging African-American middle class meant there was less need for a Benevolent Association. The Dew Drop sat vacant and silent for decades. It wasn't until 2000, when Mandeville received the building as a donation, that restoration got under way.

Today, the Dew Drop hosts a couple performances a month in the spring and fall. If you go, be prepared: there's no air-conditioning or heating, no running water, and no restrooms (you can use the building next door). The room itself can seat 100 people on backless wooden benches. The Dew Drop has no windows, only large wooden shutters that are thrown open during concerts for the many fans sitting outside on lawn chairs.

Admission is $10 and has to be paid in person, cash only. The beatitude you'll experience is free. As said by Dew Drop performer Deacon John, "The best thing about playing at a historic venue like this is that you feel the spirits permeating the room. When I get in here, I feel like my ancestors are playing backup."

Address 430 Lamarque Street, Mandeville, LA 70470, www.dewdropjazzhall.com | **Hours** Check website for performance calendar | **Tip** Getting to Mandeville will have you crossing the Causeway Bridge, the world's longest. It spans 24 miles from the south shore to the north shore. While that may sound exciting, after the first two miles, it's just another twenty-two miles of water and asphalt.

24 Dive Bar Alley

The zone for twilight festivities

New Orleans has many noted bars, from Lafitte's Blacksmith Shop (built in 1732); to the revolving Carousel Bar; to Pat O'Brien's, where the Hurricanes flow freely; to the more recently opened Saints & Sinners, owned by actor Channing Tatum. But if you have an edgier or more adventurous sensibility, you'll want to skip these popular French-Quarter taverns and head out to St. Claude Avenue in the Marigny and Bywater neighborhoods.

Lining this 15-block stretch are some of the dingiest (in a good way) and fringiest watering holes in the city. The Saturn Bar was voted best dive bar in America (yes, there is such an award). From the outside, the graffiti-covered planks covering the windows make it look like a place best avoided. Open the door and you'll be greeted by bizarre paintings, ratty booths, and six jukeboxes (none of them work).

The Hi-Ho Lounge has live music ranging from hip-hop and funk to indie rock. Their best night is Saturday, when DJ Soul Sister hosts her Hustle dance party from 11pm to 3am with a lively mix of R & B classics, Motown, and techno-pop.

Directly across the street from Hi-Ho is the Allways Lounge and Theatre, where you never know what you'll experience until you enter. The club's stage hosts a variety of acts including poetry readings, burlesque performances, Drag Bingo with Vinsantos, and, on one disturbing occasion, amateur striptease night.

Siberia features punk, metal, bounce, and Slavic bands, plus burlesque and some of the worst comics you'll ever hear. At the back of the bar, past the taxidermy deer and turkeys, is Kukhnya, a restaurant that serves Slavic soul food. Kajun's Pub offers karaoke every night, and, during football season, doles out free Jell-O shots every time the Saints score a touchdown.

An entire night in New Orleans can be filled (to the brim) bar flopping along St. Claude Avenue.

Address St. Claude Avenue from Clouet Street to Touro Street, New Orleans, LA 70117:
Saturn Bar (3067), Hi-Ho Lounge (2239), Allways Lounge & Theatre (2240), Siberia (2227),
Kajun's Pub (2256) | **Tip** In New Orleans you don't even need a bar to enjoy a stiff drink.
It's perfectly legal to walk the streets with open beer cans, filled to-go cups, or one of the
monstrously large and brightly colored Hurricane or Hand Grenade containers. A word of
warning to the uninitiated visitor: all drinking vessels must be either metal or plastic. You
cannot walk the streets carrying your booze in a glass. For that, you can receive a ticket.

25 __ Dr. Bob Folk Art

Welcoming signs inviting you to get out

Dr. Bob earned his nickname after having to deliver his only son without help from an obstetrician. Bob Shaffer, his real name, is a Dumpster-diving self-taught folk artist who's become unquestionably the most conspicuous artist in New Orleans. His "Be Nice or Leave" signs seem to be in every other gift shop and practically every dive bar, juke joint, neighborhood restaurant, and po'boy stand.

Born in 1952, Dr. Bob began his career in the arts as a woodcarver working in the French Quarter. He painted his first "Be Nice or Leave" sign simply to keep people passing by from bothering him while he sculpted. He'd first seen this phrase scribbled on a cardboard box inside a bar called Working Man's Paradise. The other side of the box read, "Nothing in this world is worth getting shot or killed over."

When people kept stealing, then buying, more of his hand-painted signs than his sculptures, Dr. Bob was nudged away from carvings to paintings. A friend convinced him to focus on signs and T-shirts with the "Be Nice or Leave" logo. Today, more than 2000 versions of the phrase are bought by collectors every year. His work has been shown in galleries across the country, even gracing the walls of the Smithsonian.

Dr. Bob works out of a studio on Chartres Street in the Bywater neighborhood, where he transforms found materials and discarded objects into art. After Hurricane Katrina, he was joined by Mike, a buddy since the seventh grade who lost his grocery business to the flood. The two make art together, with Mike often hammering old bottle caps along the frames for Dr. Bob's signs. The studio was formerly a mule barn and has retained a wonderfully raggedy and open-air atmosphere. Finished pieces and works-in-progress are stacked everywhere. A sign hung high atop the drive-in entrance advises, "Buy now before the artist dies."

Address 3027 Chartres Street, New Orleans, LA 70117, +1 504.945.2225, www.drbobart.net | **Hours** By appointment, call ahead | **Tip** Painter Simon Hardeveld's bright signs with shadowed letters surrounded by stars, stripes, and polka dots can also be spotted all over New Orleans, from the Garden District's Joey K's restaurant to Mid-City's Chickie Wah Wah. His "Shalom Y'all" and "Beware Dogs and Voodoo" have become collectible treasures. You can often find Simon working on his art in a shed on the property of Lily's Antiques on Jackson (1028 Jackson Ave).

26_ Eiffel Society

A piece of Paris in America's most Parisian city

On St. Charles Avenue, one block into the Garden District and on the riverside, you'll find a building that's very reminiscent of the Eiffel Tower. In fact, it bears more than just a striking similarity; what you see is, or was, an actual piece of the iconic Parisian monument.

In 1981, engineers discovered that the famous landmark, built for the 1889 Paris Exposition Universelle, was sagging. They decided that the restaurant, which had been added to the tower in 1937 and perched 562 feet up, was too heavy and had to be removed. A French businessman, Georges Lancelin, acquired the Restaurant de la Tour Eiffel in exchange for dismantling it. He planned to rebuild the restaurant elsewhere in Paris, but when city officials forbade him to reopen it anywhere in France, he instead sold it to American John Onorio and noted French chef Daniel Bonnot. The two paid $1.5 million to ship the disassembled restaurant to New Orleans.

Upon arrival, they were faced with 11,062 small pieces of metal with instructions written in French. The restaurant was painstakingly reconstructed and opened on Thanksgiving Day, 1986, with a charity benefit. Invitations were hand delivered on the wrappers of freshly baked loaves of French bread to guests, each of whom paid $125 to attend. Yet, just three years after its grand rebirth, the restaurant closed. Over the next couple decades, a revolving door of would-be entrepreneurs tried and failed to install restaurants and nightclubs in the building.

The structure now houses an event space and lounge called the Eiffel Society. Sitting 14 feet in the air, the 6000-square-foot venue has been used for private and ticketed parties, receptions, art installations, and fashion shows. They hold Tango Tuesdays every week, and on weekend nights, the luxury space is open to the public as a unique nightclub that features dancing, entertainment, and cocktails.

Address 2040 St. Charles Avenue, New Orleans, LA 70130, +1 504.525.2951, www.eiffelsociety.com | Hours Tue 7pm–11pm, Fri and Sat 11pm–closing | Tip While you can no longer dine at the Eiffel, Friday lunch at Galatoire's (209 Bourbon St) is a long-lasting tradition. You can spot Friday line holders – students and hobos – seated outside the restaurant beginning at 8am, paid to save a spot for those who want to secure a table on the first-come-first-serve main floor. Visiting French president Charles de Gaulle was outraged by the no-reservation policy. When he demanded, "Do you know WHO I am?" the maître d' replied, "Why yes, Mr. President. Do you know WHERE you are?"

27 Elizabeth's Restaurant
Where bacon is more than a side

You could start a fight in New Orleans arguing over where to find the best po'boy or bowl of gumbo. But when it comes to the best local breakfast, Elizabeth's is close to a unanimous choice. A *New York Times* review best summed up the appeal of this classic New Orleans joint: "The thing to love about Elizabeth's is that somebody there tried to make bacon better."

That somebody was Heidi Tull. Heidi received her culinary degree in Charleston and on her first visit to New Orleans, after ravishing the city's great restaurants, she told her husband, Joe: "I'm not leaving!" And she didn't. After working in various NOLA restaurants, Heidi finally opened her own place in 1998.

Her motto "Real Food Done Real Good" hangs on a rusted sign above Elizabeth's front door at the intersection of Gallier and Chartres. The interior walls are plastered with folk art, mostly the "Be Nice or Leave" paintings of Dr. Bob (see p. 58). The artwork gives the place a roadhouse appeal, but it's the food that inspires pilgrimages to the Bywater neighborhood. The menu includes classic grits and grillades, fried chicken livers with pepper jelly, and banana-enhanced sweet-potato waffles served with duck hash. They are also one of the few restaurants to still serve *calas*. Calas are traditional Creole deep-fried cinnamon-seasoned rice fritters dusted with powdered sugar. Slave women used to walk the Quarter with baskets of hot, fresh calas on their heads, selling them to earn money to buy their freedom.

But Elizabeth's signature – and most sinful – item is their praline bacon, prepared by baking chopped pecans, brown sugar, pork fat, and sliced bacon. It's been called the "candy of meat" and "sugary crack." Other restaurants have sought to create their own versions but Elizabeth's will forever be the Neil Armstrong or George Washington of praline bacon: they were the first. It's hell on the arteries but heaven for the soul.

Address 601 Gallier Street, New Orleans, LA 70117, +1 504.944.9272, www.elizabethsrestaurantnola.com | **Hours** Daily 8am–2:30pm (breakfast/brunch), Mon–Sat 6pm–10pm (dinner) | **Tip** There are countless other creative uses of bacon in New Orleans. Among the more seductive are the bacon-wrapped dates at Bacchanal (see p. 26), the bacon-duck-and-jalapeno poppers at Borgne (601 Loyola Ave), the maple bacon donuts at Blue Dot Donuts (4301 Canal St), and praline ice cream with bacon and butterscotch at Green Goddess (307 Exchange Pl).

28 Escape My Room
Group interaction to escape clustered internment

Escape My Room is part of an entertainment trend that is starting to show up all over the globe. It began in Japan as a real-life version of a popular video game where players used puzzle-solving to escape a digital space. Andrew Preble, son of John Preble, the eccentric founder of the Abita Mystery House (see p. 12), bumped into the escape-room movement by way of a Facebook post. He felt such an experience would be particularly fun in New Orleans when stirred with bizarre tales from the city's rich and colorful history.

The adventure begins as you enter New Orleans' main U.S. Post Office, a hideous 14-story monument to bad sixties brutalist architectural taste. On the fourth floor, you walk down a fluorescent-lit corridor past seemingly vacant offices to arrive at Suite 402. Inside is a different world, a cramped and musty 19th-century parlor filled with damask couches, threadbare drapes, and an odd collection of curios, like a diorama of Saint Louis Cemetery No. 1 and a rooster with a small alligator's head.

A hostess greets you and presents you with a form releasing them from any responsibility should you suffer harm or death. She then explains the rules. You and up to six other guests will be locked in a room next door for one hour. The group's goal is to work together to dig through chests and drawers, looking closely at odd objects and using other means to find clues, open locked boxes, and solve puzzles that will lead you to discover the one way to get out of the room. (Apparently, only 30 percent of the groups succeed before the hour is up.) There's a whole backstory about a fictional New Orleans family, the DeLaportes, and a search for their lost treasure. The voice of the hostess will occasionally come over a speaker to provide cryptic hints.

If you didn't know your fellow participants beforehand, you certainly will after you either get out or are let out.

Address 701 Loyola Avenue, New Orleans, LA 70113, +1 504.475.7580, www.escapemyroom.com | Hours Daily 10am–11:30pm; tickets can be purchased on the website | Tip If you're in New Orleans between Labor Day and November, another great place to be trapped is the Mortuary (4800 Canal St), a funeral-home-turned-haunted-house attraction that's surrounded by graveyards. What makes it especially creepy is that as you make your way through the terror-filled maze, the staff has ways to separate you from your group so that you'll turn around and suddenly find yourself all alone.

29   EvacuSpots
Getting the hell out of Dodge

Riding around town, you are likely to spot one or more 14-foot-high steel stick men, sandblasted to a high sheen and posed with an arm thrust in the air. The sculptures denote EvacuSpots, one of several measures implemented after the disaster of Hurricane Katrina in 2005 and the feared impact of Hurricane Gustav in 2008. There are 17 of these designated areas, where people can wait to be picked up by city buses and taken out of harm's way should a major hurricane threaten.

The most enduring images from Katrina were of abandoned residents – stuck on rooftops; wading through water fouled with sewage, snakes, and sometimes bloated dead bodies; and shoved into the "shelter of last resort," the Superdome, which was left without power and quickly became a hellish swamp of misery. A volunteer group, Evacuteer, formed in 2009 and devised a hurricane evacuation plan for those without the means to leave the city. They held a nationwide contest to find an artist to design statues to blazon the pickup locales. Douglas Kornfeld, a sculptor, landscape designer, and teacher from Cambridge, MA, was chosen. Kornfeld did not attempt to incorporate any of New Orleans' well-known symbols into his design; rather he created a simple human form in a hailing-a-taxi posture. As a non-New Orleanian, he didn't initially realize that this was also the traditional pose people assume at every Mardi Gras parade to solicit beads and swag from the float riders.

Each sculpture weighs 850 pounds and is made from rust-resistant steel, similar in tensile strength to the type used in bridges. Kornfeld claims his sturdy stick men should last for 100 years. During the first carnival after the statues were installed, the one on Rampart near Armstrong Park was joyfully "defaced" with beads and a sign at the top of the outstretched steel arm that read, "Throw me somethin', mister!"

Address 17 locations throughout the city; consult the EvacuSpot map at www.evacuteer.org | Tip The least-expensive shop with the largest inventory of carnival beads (more than 300 styles), masks, boas, plush toys, decorations, and novelties is Mardi Gras Spot (2812 Toulouse St), a warehouse tucked into the middle of not much else in Mid-City.

30__F & F Botanica Spiritual Supply

Ritual-aid charmacy

Walk in the front door of F & F, and you'll be overwhelmed by the largest collection of Voodoo candles you've ever seen. There are candles to help you get a job, to help win your court case, to attract money or love; there are candles to keep the law away, to cause a breakup; and, perhaps best of all, there's the all-encompassing Do What I Say candle. Like po'boys, candles can come "fully dressed." Dressed candles have been anointed with appropriate oils and herbs. They are twice as pricey, but if you really want people to Do What You Say, it's worth the extra expense.

F & F was originally named The Kingdom of the Yoruba Religion by the shop's founder, Enrique Cortéz, author of *Secretos del Oriaté de la religión yoruba*. "New" owner (of the last 30-plus years) Felix Figueroa had already been selling spiritual candles and goods around New Orleans for some time when he bought the place in 1981. With more than 6000 items on display in the store today, F & F has become the Walmart of Voodoo supplies. In addition to candles, they have essential oils, roots and herbs, books, artisan jewelry, statues of saints and demons, prayer cards, and, for some reason, Mardi Gras beads.

You can watch as people come in to describe their wants or afflictions to Felix, after which he turns to his wall of botanicals to whip up a concoction to fulfill their needs.

There are also bath powders for jinx removal, a peaceful home, and for attracting success and love. You'll even find aerosol sprays, such as the Gambling Spray (much needed before you go to the racetrack or Harrah's Casino), and those hard-to-find items like a white hair plucked from the second-born fawn of a blessed doe from the North Shore. What the white hair is supposed to do is unclear, but it's probably good to have one around "just in case."

Address 801 N Broad Street, New Orleans, LA 70119, +1 504.482.9142, www.fandfbotanica.com | **Hours** Mon, Tue, Thu–Sat 8am–5:30pm | **Tip** For one of the best psychic readings in New Orleans, steer clear of the transients lining Jackson Square and make an appointment with Cari Roy (+1 877.774.6652). Her office doesn't look any more woo-woo than a marriage counselor's or tax accountant's, but she's been rated the number-one psychic in America.

31__Fats Domino's House
Walking (or driving) to the Ninth Ward

Following 2005's Hurricane Katrina, the Ninth Ward was overrun from dawn to dusk with buses filled with tourists who'd come to gawk at the neighborhood's destruction. The community finally said "Enough!" in 2014. Today, you can only reach the area by foot, private car, cab, bike – or, if you must, the once-a-day Gray Line tour.

After the Brad Pitt-funded Make it Right homes and the few remaining signs of the hurricane's utter devastation, the most visited site in the Lower Ninth is the bright yellow house with black trim on Caffin Avenue. The large letters "FD" on the façade confirm it's the former home of music legend Fats Domino.

Fats is considered the father of R & B and a favored uncle of rock 'n' roll. Over a nearly 60-year career, he sold more than 65 million records and had 37 Top 40 hits. Only Elvis Presley sold more rock albums during the same era. Fats' Billboard chart toppers include "Blueberry Hill," "I'm Ready," and "Walking to New Orleans," among many others.

The house was both his residence and recording studio. It was also nearly the site of his death when Fats decided to ride out Hurricane Katrina and got stuck in the rising floodwaters. No one heard from him for days after the building was submerged, and many feared the worst. It was later discovered that rescue workers had airlifted him out and taken him to Dallas.

Always a shy man, Fats hasn't been onstage since performing a short set at Tipitina's in 2007. He neither tours nor travels anymore. When he was awarded the National Medal of Arts, he even turned down President Clinton's invitation to the White House, commenting, "I traveled so much, I don't have anywhere left to go."

Fats no longer lives in the Ninth-Ward dwelling, but still calls New Orleans home (he now resides in Harvey, on the West Bank). The iconic yellow house is not open for tours, but you can still drive by and rubberneck.

Address 1208 Caffin Avenue, New Orleans, LA 70117 | Hours Not open to the public; viewable from the outside only | Tip Fats' piano, removed from his home after the 2005 flood, was restored and is now on permanent display inside the Presbytère museum (51 Chartres St) as part of the exhibit "Living with Hurricanes: Katrina and Beyond."

32 Faulkner House Books

The best bookstore that won't have any best sellers

Tucked away in a narrow alley behind the St. Louis Cathedral is a bookstore that's no larger than the Pets and Nature section in a Barnes and Noble. But each volume on the packed shelves has been carefully chosen. If you're looking for a memoir by a Kardashian or the latest installment of a dystopian fantasy, you won't find it here. Faulkner House Books is a sanctuary for Literature with a capital L.

In 1990, Joe DeSalvo, ex-lawyer turned premier collector and bibliophile, and his wife, Rosemary James, a former New Orleans newscaster and noted interior decorator (you can see her work in the film *Interview with a Vampire*), bought the building that once served as William Faulkner's home and painstakingly restored the upper floors for their residence and the first floor as an elegant, chandelier-decorated bookstore.

Not yet considered the greatest American novelist of the 20th century when he resided at 624 Pirate's Alley, the young Faulkner spent his time in New Orleans the way many 20-year-olds do: mixing drinks in his bathtub, challenging friends to footraces over rooftops in the Quarter, and shooting at passersby with a BB gun. Somehow he also found the time to write a series of stories entitled *New Orleans Sketches* and the novels *Mosquitoes* and *Soldier's Pay*.

The shop often has rare and first editions of books by or about Faulkner in their ground-floor collection located on the other side of an iron gate and away from the main selling area. They've also had signed volumes by Truman Capote, Lillian Hellman, and other pillars of New Orleans literary history. More-contemporary authors, such as Willie Morris, Elizabeth Spencer, William Styron, and Barry Gifford, have all made in-store appearances.

The spirit of Faulkner, who died in 1962, is said to still occasionally drop by to make inappropriate advances every time Joe and Rosemary hire an attractive female clerk.

Address 624 Pirate's Alley, New Orleans, LA 70116, +1 504.524.2940, www.faulknerhousebooks.net | Hours Daily 10am–5pm | Tip While many cities have seen their independent bookstores slowly disappear, New Orleans still has a handful of healthy ones. In addition to Faulkner House, there's Octavia Books (513 Octavia St), Maple Street Book Shop (7529 Maple St), Garden District Book Shop (2727 Prytania St), and Blue Cypress Books (8126 Oak St). All have excellent selections of New-Orleans related titles. All sponsor readings and signings on a regular basis.

33 Fifi Mahony's
Wig paradise

Do you need an old-fashioned silver sailboat attached to a Marie Antoinette-style wig? Maybe a plastic surfer riding a wave of hair atop a vivid blue wig with hibiscus flowers planted at the bottom ready to catch his fall? How about a green wig softly teased out with peacock feathers and jewels? Fifi Mahony's has it all and more. In business since 1997, Fifi Mahony's is the place to shop for wigs, cosmetics, and anything of a sparkly nature.

Although Fifi Mahony's specializes in custom wigs, they also have row upon row of ready-to-wear wigs, such as tangerine beehives, rainbow-colored Afros, and scarlet pageboy bobs, with a selection of colors and styles so appealing that it is like an ice-cream shop for your head. Two scoops or one? With more than 100 wigs to choose from, starting around $45, customers can either shop and go, or work with a stylist for customization, and purchase accessories for extra adornment. But if you're looking for something a little more permanent, Fifi Mahony's also has a salon inside the store that offers cuts, color, extensions, and brow and makeup services. Owner Marcy Hesseling says that on many occasions, clients will love their wig color so much that they get their hair dyed to match. The shop also carries a line of traditional wigs, catering to clients with hair loss and anyone who prefers to blend in instead of stand out.

Glitter, high-quality cosmetics (Ben Nye as well as their own custom line), colorful false eyelashes, rhinestone-studded sunglasses, miniature-sequined top hats, and fascinators with a gluttony of feathers can all be found here, underneath a lavish crystal chandelier with a plaster medallion of nymphs surrounding it looking down as you browse. And if you need to validate your shopping excursion? Simply claim that you were curious to see the former home of General P. G. T. Beauregard and his son René, who lived there from 1868 to 1875.

Address 934 Royal Street, New Orleans, LA 70116, +1 504.525.4343,
www.fifimahonys.com | Hours Mon–Fri and Sun noon–6pm, Sat 11am–7pm | Tip
If looking at all of those candy-colored wigs triggers your sweet tooth, dessert shop Salon
by Sucré (622 Conti St) carries multicolored macaroons, chocolates, gelato, and pastries.

34_Frenchmen Art Market
A slip of art in a sea of music

When Bourbon Street de-evolved from premier jazz clubs to the current cluster of bars featuring loud but lumbering cover bands, Frenchmen Street became the main haven for the best New Orleans blues and jazz musicians. Live music venues line the street, literally touching one another. Every night, crowds weave in and out of the clubs from early evening until whenever A.M.

Jewelry designer and entrepreneur Katherine Erny Gaar saw her own business take a hit when the economy went south in 2009, but teamed up with John Dyer to create something bigger and better. They founded the Frenchmen Art Market initially as a pop-up for local artists to show and sell their wares during Jazz Fest, when throngs of tourists descend upon the city. Since then, the outdoor market has become a permanent fixture, the city's only nighttime bazaar, installed in an empty lot directly across from the club D.B.A. and next door to Spotted Cat.

An ever-changing roster of participants includes both known artists like New Orleans clothing designer Carrie Licciardi and skateboard artist Don Pendleton, and emerging craftsmen. You'll find for sale jewelry, photographs, paintings, sculptures, repurposed vintage clothing, and other inventive objects like hand-painted chicken feet, wine-bottle art, and wooden bow ties.

More than just a collection of artisan booths, the setting itself is inviting and pleasant. The alley is strung with small twinkling lights and features an open lounge area with tables and chairs, while the ever-present sound of music from the nearby clubs or a curbside brass band can be heard in the background.

However, a word of caution before taking photographs of the booths in a willy-nilly, helter-skelter fashion. Ask first. Some of the artists will respond to your quick snaps as though their creations are in the witness protection program.

Address 619 Frenchmen Street, New Orleans, LA 70116, +1 504.941.1149 | **Hours** Mon–Sat 7pm–1am, Sun 6pm–midnight | **Tip** Two blocks from the Art Market is Louisiana Music Factory (421 Frenchmen St). After 22 years in the French Quarter, the store relocated to the new music hub, where they offer a treasure trove of CDs and vinyl by local musicians and rare recordings by blues, zydeco, and swamp-pop artists.

35__Freret Street Boxing Gym
Fashionable fisticuffs

The Freret Street Boxing Gym has one ring, no air-conditioning, and a portable toilet out back. It's filled with folks serious about working out, jumping rope, hitting the speed bag, lifting free weights (no machines), and sparring.

In 2005, owner Mike Tata began hosting and promoting a lineup of boxing matches to the public. Staged four times a year, the Friday Night Fights have developed an almost cultlike following that includes attendees of all types, from serious boxing buffs who follow the sport to those who simply enjoy the spectacle. The fights, which take place in the street to accommodate the large crowds, feel as much like a festival as an athletic competition. Spectators are entertained by DJs, drag queens, reggae bands, burlesque performers, hot-dog-eating and bikini contests (not yet one and the same, but that can't be ruled out), dance troupes, and fans dressed up in costumes that rival Mardi Gras attire. Crowd participation is everything – many "misters" have been crowned Miss Friday Night Fights based on audience applause – and winners are often decided by the drunkest and rowdiest. The matches also attract atypical fighters. Father Kevin Wildes – Jesuit priest, president of Loyola University and holder of four master's degrees and a PhD in philosophy – has stepped into the ring, with the crowd chanting "Father, Father!" to spur him on.

For Tata, the Friday Night Fights are, financially speaking, not much more than a nonprofit event. He claims the ticket price covers little more than the costs. But Tata is in it for the fun, not the dough. Each event features eight fights (male and female) of three rounds each and six different types of entertainment. Crowds average between 1250 to 1500 people, so come early if you want to find a good seat among the encampments of regulars with their folding lawn chairs, ice coolers (the event is B.Y.O.B.), and occasional charcoal grills.

Address 1632 Oretha Castle Haley Boulevard, New Orleans, LA 70113, +1 504.895.1859, Facebook: Friday Night Fights Gym/HQ | **Hours** Gym: Mon–Fri 9am–8pm, Sat and Sun 9am–5pm. Friday Night Fights: check Facebook page for upcoming dates and location. | **Tip** Another Friday-night must-see is Miss Trixie Minx – New Orleans' premier burlesque queen – performing at midnight each week at Irvin Mayfield's Jazz Playhouse, inside the Royal Sonesta Hotel (300 Bourbon St). Minx has said of herself, "I'm just a Jewish housewife with no talent for cleaning or cooking. But, I can twirl tassels."

36 Gator Run

Keeping it cool at the zoo

When most people see a giant alligator open its massive jaws they scatter, but not at the Cool Zoo splash park at Audubon Zoo. Clearly modeled after "Spots," the white alligator at the Audubon Aquarium, this huge gator is a water slide that drops 400 gallons of water onto eager, excited kids (including grown-up kids) every 45 seconds. The 1.5-acre water park also features a spider-monkey soaker, jumping water spouts, water-spitting snakes, and custom-sculpted lion and elephant spin-and-spray big "sqwerts."

Its latest addition (in spring 2015) is Gator Run, a 750-foot lazy river that's three feet deep and ten feet wide. It takes approximately seven to ten minutes to make the full loop either in an inner tube (provided) or just floating along. On the journey you pass underneath four water cannons, two water curtains and jumping jets, and by two sand beaches. And if the animals are cooperative, you can catch glimpses of the elephants in the Asian Domain, the flock of flamingos near the South-American boardwalk, and the aviary, all from the luxury of your tube.

For those under 48 inches a life vest is required (and supplied) and for those over 21 years of age there is also beer for sale at the concession stand, along with food, toys, towels, and swim diapers. There are lockers provided as well, if you wish to stash your swimsuits and stroll around the zoo for a while.

Cool Zoo is not a mega-big water park but more of an intimate, friendly environment that caters mainly to children 12 and under, and one of its three zones is exclusively for toddlers and younger kids, although people of all ages can enjoy the sublimity of floating in the water sipping a beverage of their choice. It may seem an odd coupling to have a water park inside a zoo, but whether you're an elephant or an 11-year-old or a grizzly or a grown-up, everyone loves to beat the heat with a little splish and splash.

Address Cool Zoo in Audubon Zoo, 6500 Magazine Street, New Orleans, LA 70118, +1 504.581.4629, www.auduboninstitute.org/zoo/exhibits-and-attractions/cool-zoo | **Hours** Apr–Sep, Mon–Fri 10am–5pm, Sat and Sun 10am–6pm (after Labor Day, weekends only). | **Tip** After your trip to the zoo, visit the Audubon Butterfly Garden and Insectarium (U.S. Custom House at 423 Canal St).

37__The Germaine Cazenave Wells Mardi Gras Museum

Oysters Rockefeller with a side of sequins

If you've ever dreamed of walking into Liberace's closet just before or after eating premier Creole food, New Orleans has just the place for you.

Arnaud's is a classic restaurant, the largest in New Orleans, with 14 dining rooms. It opened in 1918 under Count Arnaud Cazenave, and his cuisine and traditions have been carried on by generations of the Casbarian family. The menu created by the count was voluminous, with 51 seafood entrees, 9 oyster appetizers alone, and 40 vegetable sides, among them potatoes prepared 16 ways. During Prohibition, Arnaud's signature item was their "coffee," served before, during, and after dinner. The count passed the running of his restaurant on to his daughter Germaine Cazenave Wells. She was known locally as just Germaine, in the same tradition as Madonna, Cher, and Beyoncé. Germaine was famously passionate about alcohol, men, and parties, and she adored the spotlight. She equated the restaurant business with theater. "It's a play in two acts," she once said, "lunch and dinner." She ruled over 22 Carnival balls and instituted her own Easter parade to show off her latest hats, with her friends, also in glitzy hats, following in horse-drawn carriages. The parade continues to this day.

When Archie Casbarian took over Arnaud's in 1978, he had the foresight to save many of Germaine's sequined hats and hand-beaded gowns. They are now displayed on the second floor of the restaurant. The small upstairs museum has more than two dozen lavish Mardi Gras costumes, including thirteen of Germaine's as well as four king's costumes worn by Count Arnaud. The collection also includes more than 70 vintage photographs, Carnival masks, and faux jewels, plus intricate krewe invitations and party favors. Viewing the cherished collection is free to the public during restaurant hours.

Address 813 Rue Bienville, New Orleans, LA 70112, +1 504.523.5433, www.arnaudsrestaurant.com/about/mardi-gras-museum | **Hours** Mon–Sat, 6pm–10:30pm, Sun 10am–2:30pm | **Tip** You can drop $20 per person to visit Mardi Gras World (1380 Port of New Orleans Pl) and it is worth it. But individual krewes also have warehouses where artisans can be found at various and unpredictable times working on floats for the coming season. While you may find a padlocked door, if you happen by a warehouse on Claiborne Ave, Bordeaux St, or elsewhere that's open, generally the artists are very welcoming.

38_Greg's Antiques
A different kind of sticker shock

Greg's Antiques, located in the French Quarter, is one of the few antiques shops in New Orleans where one experiences a different kind of sticker shock – not from high prices, but from red "sold" tags attached to many of the items. This stems from owner Greg's business philosophy: "Buy good; sell good." Greg originally came to New Orleans to photograph Hurricane Katrina's devastation, but started fixing up and selling furniture. Through a contact, he sold his first container of furniture, and then another, and another, eventually opening his own business.

Greg's main focus is furniture (primarily 1880s to 1950s European pieces), but the store also sells "junk." One can find anything down the crowded aisles: gilded antique Florentine flower chandeliers, a wide assortment of taxidermy, kimonos, stained glass, ships' helms, comic books, antique typewriters, musical instruments, vintage Mardi Gras posters, and large clown statues (proof, Greg says, that he will sell anything). Every six to eight weeks they receive a new container and in preparation they mark all their furniture down 25 percent two weeks out and 50 percent one week out. Everything is for sale – except for the commissioned art by local artists and the framed bugs.

You are going to need to take your time, not only to view everything the store has but also to maneuver yourself through some of its tight aisles – there appears to be no rhyme or reason to the placement of items except wherever they fit. And if you can't find what you want? Rent a bike from Greg and ride around the city trying to find a more interesting store with better prices (good luck). Word of warning: if you are perusing the back of the store and suddenly hear the explosive sound of glass breaking, don't be surprised by the employees' unfazed demeanor; Greg claims this and other unexplained phenomena (especially the rattling gate chain) came with the building.

Address 1209 Decatur Street, New Orleans, LA 70116, +1 504.202.8577, www.gregsantiques.com | Hours Daily 10am–10pm | Tip Check out Greg's other store, Upcycle, across the street at 1222 Decatur, where they transform junk into pieces of art (don't miss the lamps made out of musical instruments or mantel bars). The prices are based strictly on the cost of materials and labor, so chances are you will find a completely unique piece at a reasonable price.

39 __ Hansen's Sno-Bliz
New Orleans' way to beat the heat

In New Orleans, where "sno-ball" shops are as common as pizza parlors in New York, there is only one that is considered holy ground. Hansen's Sno-Bliz opened in 1939, and each year, before they reopen for the new season in May, the shop updates their hand-painted sign with the number of years they've been in business.

Master machinist Ernest Hansen built and patented an ice-shaving machine that creates a fine powder unmatched by any other in existence. His wife, Mary, a gourmet Italian cook, developed Hansen's own line of syrups to pour over the powdered ice. In addition to the common lemon, root beer, or wild cherry, you can order more exotic flavors like satsuma, ginger-cayenne, or cream of wedding cake – or mix and match several kinds. Hansen's is forever concocting new flavors, such as lavender-honey, added in 2014. For sugar overload, a Sno-Bliz may be stuffed with soft-serve ice cream or topped with marshmallow, whipped cream, or sweetened condensed milk.

Today, the family-owned shop is run by the diminutive and sweet-as-her-syrups Ashley Hansen. As Ernest and Mary's granddaughter, she's been making Sno-Bliz cups since she was 12 years old. In 2014, Ashley flew to New York to receive the "America's Classic" award from the James Beard Foundation.

If you go to Hansen's, be prepared to wait in line. Whether there are three or the more typical 30 people standing in front of you, you'll watch and wait as each one engages in friendly chitchat and swaps baby pictures. And that's kind of the point. It's a neighborhood hangout. The interior has changed very little in 75 years. The walls are lined with yellowed Polaroids and old newspaper clippings. Amid the nostalgic clutter is the sign: "There are no shortcuts to quality." That motto applies to both the Sno-Bliz you're waiting to order and the conversations you should be having in the meantime.

Address 4801 Tchoupitoulas Street, New Orleans, LA 70115, +1 504.891.9788, www.snobliz.com | **Hours** May–Oct, Tue–Sun 1pm–7pm | **Tip** Peek behind the counter to see the old cigar box used as the cash register for generations and the vintage flavored-syrup bottles, which are actually old sterilized vodka and Jack Daniels bottles collected every year during the off-season from a cousin who drank a lot.

40__Hare Krishna Temple
Culinary consciousness

If you're in New Orleans as a visitor, after a few days of subsisting on pork wrapped in bacon with a side of cracklins, you may be ready for a break from the meat sweats. For more than 30 years, the Hare Krishna Temple on Esplanade Avenue has served a vegetarian feast every Sunday night to anyone who shows up at their door. Dishes include samosas stuffed with cauliflower and peas, pakoras, assorted vegetables in a chickpea batter, pushpanna rice with nuts and spices, puris, a tortilla-like fried wheat bread, and various curries and cheeses. Desserts can be kheer, a rice pudding made with sweetened condensed milk, or burfi, a sweet with a vanilla fudge consistency.

Best of all, and most surprisingly, the entire meal is absolutely free. More than free: you can bring Tupperware containers to take food home.

Although some people partaking in the buffet will be homeless or in desperate need, what makes the Sunday "soup kitchen" unique is that the weekly crowd also includes many neighborhood residents, university students, and some regulars who just enjoy being part of a community and meeting new people.

The dinners began when the founder and spiritual master of the International Society for Krishna Consciousness, Srila Prabhupada, saw children fighting in the street over scraps of food. He told his yoga students no one should go hungry and quickly set up a network of free food kitchens, which grew in scope to become 350 Hare Krishna temples across the world. The Sunday feast, called *prasadam*, embodies an important tenet of the faith.

The New Orleans Hare Krishna community has about 300 members. Immediately after Katrina, the Krishnas joined the Food for Life program to serve more than 5000 free meals. For the Sunday dinners, there will be chanting, dancing, and philosophizing, but no one will care if you're just there for noshing.

Address 2936 Esplanade Avenue, New Orleans, LA 70119, +1 504.638.3244, www.iskconcenters.com/new-orleans | **Hours** Sun 6pm–9pm | **Tip** If you'd rather pay for your dinner, close to the temple is New Orleans' best Spanish restaurant, Lola's (3312 Esplanade Ave). If you love garlic, you will love Lola's. Surprisingly, there are only two Spanish restaurants in New Orleans; curious for a city that was under Spanish rule for nearly 40 years.

41__The Healing Center

The mall for people who hate malls

The New Orleans Healing Center is a hip, not-quite-a-mall in a 55,000-square-foot building. Painted bright orange, it can't be missed. The center is dedicated to promoting physical, emotional, intellectual, artistic, and environmental well-being.

It houses some things you might expect from its name and mission: yoga classes, a health club, and a food co-op. There's also a closet-sized shop called Two Guys Cutting Hair, which is two guys, Adikus and Trent, who cut hair (brilliantly, according to reviews), and a boutique florist, Arbor House, run by two other guys who met as members of Mystic Mardi Krewe, a group known for their elaborate costumes and balls. Fatoush is the lone restaurant in the Center. They serve Middle Eastern food and, in keeping with the don't-call-it-a-mall theme, claim to offer a path to inner peace that travels directly through the stomach.

But the calling cards that bookend the center are a Voodoo shop called the Island of Salvation Botanica at the front, and Cafe Istanbul, a performance center, at the back.

Salvation Botanica's owner, Sallie Ann Glassman, once a nice Jewish girl from Maine, is one of the few white women ordained as Voodoo priestesses. Her store is stocked with "real" religious supplies, medicinal herbs, and Haitian artwork, as opposed to the made-in-China gris-gris and Voodoo dolls found in many gift shops. She also performs readings on the premises. Just outside Glassman's door in the lobby is the International Marie Laveau Shrine, a nine-foot-tall statue of the Voodoo queen sculpted by Ricardo Pustanio.

Café Istanbul is a 3,800-square-foot hall that fosters and promotes performance art in New Orleans. They host live music, theater, dance, comedy, and film screenings. Monthly events include shows by the Moth, an open-mic storytelling competition, and the Goodnight Show, New Orleans' take on Garrison Keillor's *A Prairie Home Companion*.

Address 2372 St. Claude Avenue, New Orleans, LA 70117, +1 504.940.1130, www.neworleanshealingcenter.org | **Hours** Tue – Sat 10am – 6pm | **Tip** Nearby is a war monument for people who don't want to stand in line to pay $24 for the massive World War II Museum in the Warehouse District. A carved stone victory arch (Burgundy St, between Alvar and Pauline Sts) honors residents of the Ninth Ward who served in World War I. The arch was the first memorial for the Great War in the United States.

42__Holt Cemetery

The unknown grave for the well-known Father of Jazz

Holt is New Orleans' most unkempt and haphazard cemetery. Founded in 1879, originally it was a potter's field, or indigent cemetery for those who couldn't afford burial. Unlike the more famous aboveground cemeteries, here the graves – some shaded by a few beautiful old oak trees – are mostly beneath the earth.

There are two tributes in Holt to Buddy Bolden, credited as the Father of Jazz, but no one knows the site of his actual grave. He was a victim of acute alcohol psychosis and schizophrenia, and spent the last 24 years of his life in the Louisiana State Insane Asylum. Before his decline, Buddy had developed a looser, more improvised version of ragtime to which he added blues and funk. One of his early hits, "Funky Butt," totally changed the musical landscape. He is also credited with the invention of the so-called "Big Four" – the first syncopated bass drum rhythm to deviate from the standard march beat. The second half of the Big Four is the pattern commonly known as *habanera* rhythm, or basically, the "New Orleans Sound." Thus, Buddy Bolden, buried who-knows-where in Holt Cemetery, can be considered perhaps the most important musician in NOLA history, and quite possibly all of America.

While not finding Buddy's grave, you will find a bizarre landscape of all manner of stuffed animals, dime-store-quality statues of Mary and St. Francis, singing cherubs, plastic flowers, and carpet remnants strewn throughout the cemetery. There are unconfirmed tales of human bones that have worked their way up to the surface. In a sea of wonderful hand-carved and handmade headstones made by loved ones of the deceased, Miss Thelma Lowe has a coveted Zulu coconut on her grave. Many epitaphs are written in magic marker; a few others are spelled out in mosaics made with ceramic shards. One Emily Lorraine's headstone states that she died in 2004 and was "bone" on June 20, 1947.

Address 527 City Park Avenue, New Orleans, LA 70119, +1 504.658.3781 | Hours Mon−Fri 8am−2:30pm, Sat 8am−noon | Tip If looking for bones and unmarked graves leaves you hungry, there's a classic 24−hour burger joint practically across the street. Bud's Broiler (500 City Park Ave) opened in 1956 and became famous for Bud Saunders' "secret Hickory Smoke Sauce."

43 Hong Kong Food Market
A ridiculous name for a remarkable emporium

If you believe Anthony Bourdain or *Saveur* magazine, New Orleans is the culinary capital of America. Visitors come to devour Creole or Cajun cuisines and regional seafood like crawfish, oysters, and catfish. What is less known is that the Big Easy also offers the best Vietnamese food in the country.

Prior to 1975, there were 15,000 Vietnamese in all of the United States – today there are 15,000 in New Orleans alone. Toward the end of the Vietnam War, thousands fled their native country and came to America. Perhaps because, like Vietnam, New Orleans has strong French influences, a subtropical climate, and swampy terrain, many of these immigrants were drawn to the city. Most settled on the West Bank, locally called the Wank. The first Vietnamese restaurant in New Orleans was Hong Lan, which opened in 1976 but closed just two years later because business was actually too successful and the owner grew tired of working 18-hour days.

Today, it's hard to keep track of all the Vietnamese restaurants in NOLA. The Wank remains the heartland, with classics like Pho Tau Bay and Dong Phuong. It's also where you'll find the poorly named Hong Kong Market – a vast Walmart-sized retail sea of Vietnamese foods, frequented by both local chefs and home cooks. Here you can buy produce (kimchi to durian), fish, meat (including duck tongues), sauces (nuoc mam), and don't forget your mung-bean starch.

The aisles display more varieties of noodles than Baskin-Robbins has ice-cream flavors. The back of the store sells fresh shrimp and oysters next to even fresher catfish and tilapia, still swimming in tanks. There are several stands where you can dine inside the massive store. Saigon Grill & Deli will hack up an entire roasted duck right in front of you, Pho Danh 4 serves hot bowls of noodles, and you can wash them down with teas from Mr. Bubble's, in flavors like honeydew with rainbow tapioca and avocado.

Address 925 Behrman Highway, Gretna, LA 70056, +1.504.394.7075, www.hongkongmarketnola.com | Hours Daily 8am–8:30pm | Tip More recent years have seen Vietnamese restaurants migrate from the Wank to the more accessible Uptown and Carrollton neighborhoods. Among them, Cafe Minh in Mid-City (4139 Canal St) is more upscale and a favorite of local food critics. Lilly's Café (1813 Magazine St) is a tiny spot in the Lower Garden District with no more than five or six always-filled tables, often with a celebrity chef like Tom Colicchio or restaurateur like Upperline's JoAnn Clevenger.

44 House of Broel
Dresses, dollhouses, and frog legs

The Victorian mansion known as House of Broel is one of countless antebellum homes that line St. Charles Avenue. Originally built in 1850, the house was lifted by William Renaud in 1884 to add a spacious new first floor for parties and other social events. Under the longtime ownership of Bonnie Broel, it has become an extremely popular wedding venue.

For many years it was also where the vast majority of New Orleans brides and young women purchased their wedding, Mardi Gras, and prom gowns designed by Ms. Broel. In 1995, local author Anne Rice staged her own funeral wearing one of Ms. Broel's wedding dresses. She lay down in a coffin in Lafayette No. 1 and was later taken by horse-drawn hearse to her book signing at the Garden District Book Shop.

What truly sets this unusual house apart is what you'll find upstairs; the Dollhouse Museum features a number of Ms. Broel's meticulously detailed miniatures of Victorian, Tudor, and plantation-style houses (complete with furniture and tiny people engaged in various activities) built to scale. The centerpiece is a 10-foot-tall, 12-foot-wide three-story turn-of the-century Russian palace with almost thirty rooms. Other models include an English hunting lodge, a fairy hut, an Asian art shop, a bridal salon, and a cowboy-themed brothel. Encompassing more than 3000 square feet, the collection of tiny houses is, as far as Ms. Broel knows, the largest miniature museum created by a single person.

And then, apropos of nothing, the second floor also includes a frog collection. The exhibit is an homage to frog farming – Ms. Broel's father was the founder of the American Frog Canning Company and even penned a handbook on frog farming. Here you can see vintage cans of frog legs on display and all varieties of frog figurines, among other frog-related objects.

Address 2220 St. Charles Avenue, New Orleans, LA 70130, +1 504.522.2220, www.houseofbroel.com | **Hours** Tours by appointment only | **Tip** More miniatures may be seen at the Basin Street Visitors Center (501 Basin St). Inside the 105-year-old restored old Southern Railway Station you'll find a scale model of the City of New Orleans.

45_ House of Dance & Feathers

Street cred in a shed

Ronald W. Lewis, a retired streetcar worker and lifelong resident of the Lower Ninth Ward, has turned his backyard into what is perhaps New Orleans' most eccentric museum. And in this city, which features a Voodoo museum, a haunted pharmacy museum, and the Museum of the American Cocktail, that's saying something.

Mr. Ronald, as he's known, is also president of the Big Nine Social Aid & Pleasure Club, the former council chief of the Mardi Gras Indian tribe the Choctaw Hunters, and the former king of Krewe de Vieux. These benevolent societies were uniquely founded in New Orleans in the 1800s by different ethnic groups to help dues-paying members defray health-care costs, funeral expenses, and financial hardship. They also fostered a sense of unity in the community, performed charitable works, and hosted social events and parades.

Mardi Gras Indians work an entire year on their elaborate outfits of feathers with West-African beading to wear them on only two occasions: Mardi Gras and St. Joseph's Day. A suit can cost thousands of dollars and weigh upwards of 100 pounds. One day, while Mr. Ronald was working on his costumes, his wife, Minnie, came home to find feathers, beads, and memorabilia strewn all over the house. "I can't take this anymore!" she announced. So he took all his "stuff" out back to a shed. Kids in the neighborhood started calling it a museum and Mr. Ronald christened his outbuilding the House of Dance & Feathers, his personal tribute to the New Orleans parade culture and Mardi Gras Indians.

The museum officially opened in 2003, only to be flooded by Katrina two years later and rebuilt through Mr. Ronald's resolve. Call ahead to schedule a time to meet with him. He is as much (or more) the reason to visit as all of his masks, suits, figures, books, photographs, and other quirky curios. As posted on his shed and website, "Come in a stranger, leave a friend!"

Address 1317 Tupelo Street, New Orleans, LA 70117, +1 504.957.2678,
www.houseofdanceandfeathers.org | Hours Visits by appointment only | Tip The
nearby Lower Ninth Ward Living Museum (1235 Deslonde St), features illuminating
exhibits that detail the neighborhood's history of social activism, from when the Lower
Ninth was an enclave of former slaves, through desegregation, and up to the devastation
caused by Hurricane Katrina.

46__Ignatius J. Reilly Statue
Watching for signs of bad taste

Many cities have theme songs, like Tony Bennett's "I Left My Heart in San Francisco" or Frank Sinatra's "New York, New York." New Orleans has not one, but many signature tunes, delivered by great musicians ranging from Louis Armstrong to Dr. John. The city does, however, have one definitive theme novel: John Kennedy Toole's *A Confederacy of Dunces.*

Toole committed suicide at age 31, depressed by having failed to find a publisher for his book. His mother took up the cause after his death and literally forced her son's manuscript upon Walker Percy, a Southern literary giant. Expecting the worst, when Percy finally dipped into the pages, he said he felt "a prickle of interest, then a growing excitement, and finally an incredulity: surely it was not possible that it was so good." He convinced LSU Press to publish the novel. It is now considered a canonical work of modern literature and has been translated into 35 languages.

The novel centers on Ignatius J. Reilly, a well educated but utterly slothful 30-year-old man living with his mother in New Orleans, barely employable (he was fired as a hot-dog vendor for eating the inventory), and railing at the vulgarity of modern culture, up to and including canned peas. In the novel, Ignatius states, "I am at the moment writing a lengthy indictment against our century. When my brain begins to reel from my literary labors, I make an occasional cheese dip." He's been called a modern-day Don Quixote – eccentric, idealistic, and overwhelmingly delusional.

A bronze statue of Ignatius J. Reilly, sculpted by William Ludwig, is located under the clock on the 800 block of Canal Street. The statue depicts Ignatius in the opening scene of the novel, as he waits for his mother under the clock, clutching a Werlein's shopping bag, dressed in a hunting cap, flannel shirt, baggy pants, and scarf, "studying the crowd of people for signs of bad taste."

Address 819 Canal Street, New Orleans, LA 70112 | Tip There is supposedly a curse on filming an adaptation of *A Confederacy of Dunces*. John Belushi, John Candy, and Chris Farley were all touted for the Ignatius role. All died at an early age before fulfilling it. John Waters had been interested in directing a screen adaptation starring Divine, but the actor and drag queen likewise died young. Ignoring the curse, Zach Galifianakis is the most recent actor to consider the role.

47__James H. Cohen & Sons
Buying a piece of history

Having opened in 1898, Cohen & Sons spans three centuries and five generations of ownership, making it the oldest family-owned business of any kind in the United States. The shop started out as an vintage emporium, but because of grandson Jimmie's passion for antique weaponry and rare currency, the armoires and rugs were gradually pushed out, nudging the store into the fantastic specialized store you'll find today.

Jimmie's fervor for swords, guns, and especially coins was sparked when a customer showed up one day with a Confederate half dollar, originally struck in 1861 at the New Orleans Mint – one of only four such coins in the world. Jimmie carried the treasured coin in his pocket for weeks, checking it constantly. He finally sold it for a hefty five-figure price, making him a star among numismatics. Today the coin is worth over $1 million.

Now in their 60s, Jimmie's sons, Steve and Jerry, began working in the store after school and on weekends when they were kids. The Cohens took the boys on the road to trade shows and antiquing in Europe, instilling in them a sense of history and an eye for spotting rare and exceptional relics. If you bring Steve and Jerry any coin, sword, or antique rifle, you'll receive a PhD-worthy thesis on the object.

Cohen & Sons also provides a home for Don Weil's marvelous creations. For many years, Mr. Weil ran a shop (now closed) in the French Quarter called Le Petit Soldier, where you could buy tiny metal Civil War soldiers or members of the Roman Guard. But most appealing were little Marie Laveaus, Mardi Gras Indians, and a figure of Napoleon and Josephine holding hands, seated on a couch.

You can buy the tin figurines as well as antique weaponry and currency online. Though it feels a little weird to have a $3000 French mounted breastplate or a $5000 uncut sheet of Confederate 10-dollar notes as items you can just "Add to Cart."

Address 437 Royal Street, New Orleans, LA 70130, +1 504.522.3305, www.shop. cohenantiques.com | Hours Mon–Sat 9:30am–5pm | Tip The building that houses Cohen & Sons is the former home of a Creole apothecary owned by Antoine Amedee Peychaud. Peychaud used to treat friends to homemade brandy toddies, which he prepared using a jigger, then known as a *coquetier*. The word became bastardized into "cocktail." Thus, on this spot where you can today buy a pistol, the world's first cocktail was born.

48 __ Jazz Brunch at Atchafalaya
DIY *Bloody Marys*

The jazz brunch was the brainchild of restaurateur Dickie Brennan Sr. He was standing in the lobby of a grand hotel in London, watching a quiet sedate breakfast being served in the dining room while a trio of musicians played on the other side of the lobby. A lightbulb went on in his head. Dickie ran back to his hotel room and called his sister Ella in New Orleans. "Ella! Listen to this! Jazz brunch!" It was three o'clock in the morning in Louisiana and Ella questioned how much he had been drinking. But when he returned home, he gave the idea a shot. The Jazz Brunch at Commander's Palace was an immediate success, and in fact made the restaurant one of the most profitable in the world, as long lines waited (and still wait) to pay good money for meals built around very inexpensive eggs.

In the city that invented the jazz brunch and where the daytime Sunday meal is one of the big socio-cultural events of the week, today you have many options in addition to Commander's Palace; Arnaud's, Antoine's, and the Crystal Room inside Le Pavillon Hotel, to name just a few of the most popular. But one of the best newcomers and lesser-known spots (so far) is the high-energy jazz brunch at Atchafalaya Restaurant in the Lower Garden District. Every Sunday, the joint is jumping with lively diners and live musicians who might be playing jazz or blues or funk, depending on the weekend.

Their menu features house-brunch specialties eggs Rockefeller, bananas Foster French toast, duck hash, grits and grillades, and their most popular dish, eggs Tremé, which includes boudin cake. Their top-billing item, however, is an entire buffet set up exclusively for making Bloody Marys. You can choose either a traditional tomato base or a green base made with tomatillos and green tomatoes. To spice up and customize your cocktail, the buffet features a huge array of vegetables and less-common garnishes, like bacon and shrimp.

Address 901 Louisiana Avenue, New Orleans, LA 70115, +1 504.891.9626, www.atchafalayarestaurant.com | **Hours** Sat and Sun 10am–2:30pm | **Tip** In a city made for Sunday Bloody Marys, "the best" spots include Pat O'Brien's (718 St. Peter St) with their proprietary Bloody Mary mix and spiced-green-bean-and-lime-wedge garnish; the Avenue Pub (1732 St. Charles Ave) with their cucumber vodka Bloody Marys; and not surprisingly, Commander's Palace, who make their mix in-house every single day, adjusting ingredients to include the day's freshest produce.

49__The Jazz Collection
A brass menagerie

In the 18th and 19th centuries, immigrants from many countries flowed into the port city of New Orleans and created its unique culture. The French and Spanish had the most influence as far as food, architecture, and customs. Germany, Ireland, and Italy also played a part. Musically, the greatest contributions unquestionably came from Africa, as slaves brought chants and instruments that were the basis of what would evolve into jazz.

New Orleans' Buddy Bolden is widely considered the Father of Jazz. In his footsteps came a quick succession of innovators: Jelly Roll Morton, Kid Ory, Bunk Johnson, King Oliver, and most famously, Louis Armstrong, whose remarkable trumpet playing and distinctive raspy voice made him jazz's ambassador to the world.

It is fitting, some might say necessary, that a jazz museum was finally founded in New Orleans in 1948. At that time, many of the early jazz greats were getting on in years, and had their memorabilia, photos, and recordings not been gathered, much of the history of the genre would have been lost.

The museum is now housed at the Old U.S. Mint, where the sound of jazz music can be heard throughout the exhibition halls. The collection comprises many original instruments including George Lewis' metal clarinet, Fats Domino's baby grand Steinway, and the star attraction, the horn on which Louis Armstrong first learned to play, which has an interesting backstory. When Armstrong (1901–1971) was just 12 years old, he was arrested for shooting a gun into the air on New Year's Eve and sent to the Colored Waifs Home. It was during his time there that he was taught how to play the cornet. The widow of the home's administrator donated the instrument to the Jazz Museum in 1962. When Armstrong visited the museum in 1965, he confirmed the horn was his, based on "the grooves he had cut into the mouthpiece."

AddressThe Old U.S. Mint, 400 Esplanade Avenue, New Orleans, LA 70116, +1 504.568.6993, www.musicatthemint.org | **Hours** Tue–Thu noon–4pm, Sat 10am–4pm | **Tip** Andrew Jackson advocated construction of the U.S. Mint in 1835 to finance western expansion. The building has served as a federal jail, coast guard station, and the mint that created Confederate dollars, U.S. dollars, and ten-dollar notes in French, or *dix*, which gave the region its nickname, "Dixie."

50___Josie Arlington's Tomb
The lady burnishes

It's common to find tourists stacked three deep around Marie Laveau's grave, in St. Louis No. 1, New Orleans' most celebrated cemetery. After Elvis', in Memphis, hers is the second most visited gravesite in the States. By contrast, Josie Arlington's former tomb, in the Metairie Cemetery, is largely ignored, but her story is as rich as any.

During the early 1900s, Storyville was a section of New Orleans zoned for legalized prostitution, and Josie Arlington was its most renowned madam. She staffed her opulent bordello, the Chateau Lobrano d'Arlington, with educated women from Europe and trained them in the arts of every fetish a man might have. She charged a then extravagant fee of $5 per hour when the going rate was just 22 cents.

In 1917 the federal government shut down Storyville. The closure was made over the objections of the city. Mayor Martin Behrman pronounced, "You can make prostitution illegal, but you can't make it unpopular." By this time, Josie had already acquired great wealth. Learning that she intended to be buried in the exclusive Metairie Cemetery, a cartel of society wives – mortified that such a woman would be buried near their husbands or fathers – sought, unsuccessfully, to block her. Josie responded, "I wonder how many of these ladies know their husbands visit me weekly."

In 1914 Josie was interred near the front of the cemetery in a beautiful red granite tomb with carved burning urns and a bronze statue of a woman reaching for the door. Two gravediggers swore they witnessed the statue walk off one night. Others have claimed they've seen the stone torches burst into real flames.

Arlington's remains were moved to another secret location in the cemetery sometime after her death, and her exact whereabouts remain unknown. The family name on the original gravesite is now, ironically, Morales, the Spanish word for "moral character."

Address Metairie Cemetery, 5100 Pontchartrain Boulevard, New Orleans, LA 70124, +1 504.486.6331 | Hours Daily 7:30am–5:30pm | Tip At the nearby Odd Fellows Rest Cemetery (5055 Canal St), the elaborately designed side gate is said to possess spiritual powers. Walk up to the gate and say the name of a dead loved one five times and they will purportedly show up to answer your questions from the other side.

51 Kayaking on the Bayou
Commuting with nature

For many years, Bayou St. John served as not more than a sliver of an urban park where people sometimes picnicked or just sat and looked at the water. More recently, residents and visitors have discovered kayaking the bayou as both a pleasant leisure-time activity and a fun alternative way to tour the city. Kayaking will take you through a number of neighborhoods and past the Spanish Custom House; the historic Pitot House, a plantation dating back to the 1700s; City Park; and St. Louis Cemetery No. 3. You're also likely to see a number of birds, from great blue herons to pelicans, and in the evening, our annoying nutria (see Tip).

A sea of kayaks will jam the bayou for events like the 4th of July Krewe of Kolosos Flotilla Parade. The term "parade" is used loosely, as paddlers in outrageous costumes cluster, meander, and bump into one another's decorated boats. They are joined on the water by the Disco Amigos dance troupe on their floating barge.

You can rent kayaks at several places in the city. Bayou Paddlesports (www.bayoupaddlesports.com) meets you at a launch area right on the bayou. The company also hosts events such as moonlight paddles and an annual Earth Day regatta.

For guided tours, Kayak-iti-yat (www.kayakitiyat.com) has become the most popular outfit. They offer three tours for various levels of vigor and experience. Their intermediate three-hour Bayou Bienvenue tour focuses on the waterway's rich ecosystem, including gators. Their website will lure you in or send you running when they state the tour requires "the type of person to perceive unexpected challenges as added adventure and not a buzzkill. There are no civilized bathrooms, and no breaks or possibility of exiting the kayaks mid-tour."

Being that it's New Orleans, any tour can be turned into a booze cruise: they bring the paddle, you bring the booze.

Address Bayou St. John, New Orleans, LA | **Tip** Pretty much every body of water in New Orleans will have nutria swimming around. The nutria is a beaver-looking animal with bright orange teeth and a ratlike tail. The females have nipples on their backs for babies to cling to as they swim in murky waters. This unpleasant vermin was brought here from South America for its fur. In an effort to control its population, the state now offers a bounty to hunters of $5 for each nutria tail they deliver.

52 Kermit's Mother-in-Law Lounge

Bar of the "Emperor of the Universe"

Ernie K-Doe (1936–2001) was a one-hit wonder but a lifetime of wonderment. Even in New Orleans, where eccentrics are relished as much as accepted, K-Doe was in a class by himself. He began recording when he was 15 years old. Ten years later, his song "Mother-in-Law" became a No. 1 Billboard hit. The tune was a tribute to his real-life mother-in-law, about whom he once said, "Her name was Lucy. Should have been Lucifer." With the British invasion, K-Doe's style took a backseat to groups like the Rolling Stones and he stopped making records. For a while he drank heavily and was homeless.

K-Doe made a comeback of sorts in the 1980s when WWOZ radio gave him his own show. He assaulted the airwaves with rants about whatever popped into his head. When the station had to sell, new management was less enamored of K-Doe's on-air stream of semi-consciousness. He was back on the streets.

Sometime during this period K-Doe met Antoinette Dorsey Fox, who would become his wife. Antoinette pulled him back from the brink. She made him flashy outfits: shiny suits, feathered hats, and floor-length capes. In 1996, she opened the Mother-in-Law Lounge and stuffed it with photographs and paintings of K-Doe and a jukebox filled with his songs. It became a hot spot.

When K-Doe died, Antoinette commissioned a mannequin of her husband. The statue most often stood onstage in the club, but she'd sometimes take it out on the town, having it join her at a table in Galatoire's or on a parade float. When she died, in 2009, K-Doe's mannequin followed along behind her hearse in a mule-drawn carriage.

The juke joint was bought by star trumpet player Kermit Ruffins and reopened as Kermit's Mother-in-Law Lounge in 2014. With its extravagantly painted murals, the building is impossible to miss.

Address 1500 N Claiborne Avenue, New Orleans, LA 70116. (Like the juke joint it is, four phone numbers are posted online. Three didn't ring through. The fourth was a recorded voice saying, "What's the case Ace? No one can take your call.") | **Hours** It's open when it's open, and not open when it's closed. | **Tip** Kermit Ruffins, who's close to local royalty, can be heard most Saturday nights at the Little Gem (445 Rampart St), Friday nights at the Blue Nile (532 Frenchmen St), Tuesdays at Bullet's Sports Bar (2441 A. P. Tureaud Ave), and some Sundays at his own Mother-in-Law Lounge.

53 Killer Poboys
The richest po'boys

The famous po'boy was invented by two brothers, Benny and Clovis Martin. They were streetcar conductors who went on to open a sandwich shop near the French Market in 1921. During the railroad strike of 1929, they served their picketing friends and former coworkers, or "poor boys," a sandwich consisting of gravy inside a small loaf of French bread.

Today, po'boys are made with shrimp, oysters, roast beef, meatballs, duck debris, and pretty much anything else you can think of, and they're served at dozens, if not hundreds, of joints around New Orleans. Parkway Bakery, in Mid-City, wins most of the "best of" competitions. Domilise, in Uptown, wins those Parkway does not. Johnny's, on St. Louis Street, is probably the most visited in town because of their convenient French Quarter location.

One of the newer contenders, Killer Poboys, was opened in 2012 by April Bellows and Cam Boudreaux as a pop-up in the back of the divey Erin Rose Bar (whose motto is "Local prices. Local chaos. Local love"). Boudreaux's expressed intent is to "explore new traditions for our city's iconic sandwich." Many now consider Killer's unconventional take on New Orleans' signature sandwich (locals say "sammitch") head and tail above the rest. Boudreaux was previously a chef at Arnaud's, one of the city's classic restaurants, and his mastery of global flavors and appreciation for regionally sourced ingredients comes through in every messy bite.

Their most popular po'boy is the Dark & Stormy, made from naturally raised pork bellies from Beeler's Farms, then marinated for 12 hours in Steen's syrup, real ginger, and dark rum. Another highlight of the small but seasonal menu is a seared Gulf shrimp po'boy, with marinated radish, carrot, cucumber, herbs, and sriracha aioli.

A word of warning about the potato salad; it's great, but made with enough Zatarain's mustard to clear your sinuses.

Address Erin Rose Bar, 811 Conti Street, New Orleans, LA 70112, +1 504.252.6745, www.killerpoboys.blogspot.com | **Hours** Wed–Mon noon–midnight | **Tip** If the bartender on duty at Erin Rose is burly, bearded, shaved-headed, and has sleeve tattoos, stop and talk with him. That's Murf Reeves, also a disc jockey for WWOZ radio and a passionate and expert storytelling apostle for New Orleans. He can give you another 111 places not to miss that aren't listed in this book.

54 Lafcadio Hearn's House

The inventor of New Orleans slept here

Nestled among the tall steel-and-glass buildings of the Tulane Medical Center is an out-of-place brick house that was once the home of 19th-century journalist Lafcadio Hearn (1850–1904), dubbed "the inventor of New Orleans."

Hearn, who was born in Greece, was abandoned by his mother and raised by Irish relatives who shipped him off to the States at 19. In Cincinnati, he took odd jobs, lived in a stable, read voraciously, and eventually became a self-taught writer. He started penning profiles for the *Cincinnati Enquirer*, but was forced to leave Ohio for New Orleans in 1877, when he broke a state law by marrying a biracial woman.

Drawn to others on the fringe, Hearn and New Orleans formed a perfect marriage of misfits. His exotic stories about his new adopted city became regular pieces in *Scribner's*, *Cosmopolitan*, and *Harper's Bazaar*. It was Hearn who first wrote down the folklore of the unique local cuisine in his verbosely named book, *La Cuisine Creole: A Collection of Culinary Recipes, From Leading Chefs and Noted Creole Housewives, Who Have Made New Orleans Famous for Its Cuisine*. It was Hearn who also detailed for outsiders the customs of the Voodoo religion. And it was Hearn who painted word pictures of New Orleans as the most exotic city in America: "There are few who can visit her for the first time without delight; and few who can ever leave her without regret; and none who can forget her strange charm when they have once felt its influence."

Ever the wanderer, Hearn moved to Martinique in 1887, then settled in Japan. His former NOLA neighborhood grew seedy and his residence became a dingy flophouse. The property was eventually bought and restored by Saints linebacker Pat Swilling. Richard Scribner, an LSU professor, then took ownership and through his efforts the house was designated a historic landmark and added to the National Register of Historic Places.

Address 1565 Cleveland Street, New Orleans, LA 70112 | **Hours** Not open to the public; viewable from the outside only | **Tip** Note that the modern buildings surrounding Hearn's former house are not the towering monoliths one finds in many American cities. Because New Orleans is resting on a swamp, there are no real skyscrapers. Donald Trump learned why when he endeavored to erect a tower but was informed by architects that a 70-story building in New Orleans would require a 50-story profit-sucking foundation or it would sink. The Donald abandoned his plan.

55___Lakefront Airport

An Art Deco museum masquerading as an airport

After 90 years of municipal squabbles and natural disasters, the Lakefront Airport sits as a wonderfully preserved exhibition of the Art Deco age. In 1929, Abraham Shushan, a politician, businessman, and a bit of a shyster, teamed up with then governor Huey Long to push through their vision for a modern airport. The two spent $3 million to pump out 6 million cubic yards of water to build the airport on a newly formed jetty where a portion of Lake Pontchartrain had been. The land formerly underwater was in the public domain, which meant that anti-Long political factions had no say or control.

Christened the Shushan Airport when it opened in 1934, it was the first combined land and seaplane air terminal in the world. The grand Atrium has a terrazzo floor and is lined with aviation-themed murals by Spanish-American artist Xavier Gonzalez. There are ornamental touches everywhere you turn, from the neon arrow pointing to the Walnut Room to a retro bank of phone booths.

A controversial sculpture / fountain by Enrique Alférez sits out front and depicts the four seasons as three women and a man, all nude. In 1936 it was deemed indecent and city officials demanded the endowed male statue have his genitalia chiseled off. Alférez refused and stood guard every night with a rifle to ward off vandals. Eleanor Roosevelt finally stepped in and demanded the sculpture remain as it was created.

More controversy followed in 1939 when Shusan was indicted and convicted on various charges of theft and fraud. In response, the board changed the name to Lakefront Airport. However, they had a much harder time removing Abe's name from all the surfaces of the terminal. In a Donald Trump-like way, he had crazily etched his name in the lavatories, on the doors, in the wall tiles, and even on the pavement outside. One board member admitted defeat: "We haven't got the kind of money it would take to get Abe off everything."

Address 6001 Stars & Stripes Boulevard, New Orleans, LA 70126, +1 504.243.4010, www.lakefrontairport.com | **Tip** You can dine at Messina's Runway Cafe in the airport lobby. They are open from 8am to 3pm, serving local dishes such as eggs hussard, shrimp and grits, po'boys, and signature homemade sweet-potato biscuits.

56 The LaLaurie Mansion
The house of unspeakable horrors

The grisly legend of what once went on inside the house at 1140 Royal Street has haunted generations of New Orleanians and is the inspiration for the hit TV series *American Horror Story*. In the 1830s, Madame Delphine LaLaurie, a New Orleans socialite, and her husband, Dr. Louis LaLaurie, were by all outward appearances a well-respected couple in the community. But behind closed doors, they exercised their savagely sadistic inclinations: Madame LaLaurie is said to have tortured and murdered an untold number of slaves in the most horrific and unthinkable ways.

The couple's heinous acts were finally revealed on April 10, 1834, when their house cook purposefully set a blaze and firemen were called to the mansion. According to Jeanne deLavigne's *Ghost Stories of Old New Orleans* (written in 1946), the responding firemen found "male slaves, stark naked, chained to the wall, their eyes gouged out, their fingernails pulled off by the roots; others had their joints skinned and festering." *Journey Into Darkness: Ghosts and Vampires of New Orleans* (written 52 years later, in 1998) by Kalila Katherina Smith, added even more explicit details about the state of the victims, including one who "had her arms amputated and her skin peeled off in a circular pattern, making her look like a human caterpillar," and another who had had her limbs broken and reset "at odd angles so she resembled a human crab."

Since the LaLauries' escape to France, subsequent owners have reported many ghost sightings. The house's most famous proprietor was actor Nicolas Cage, who possessed the mansion for years but supposedly never lived there. One evening, a tour guide was standing before the property relaying the nasty tales to an assembled crowd. When the guide mentioned that Cage had never dared to stay overnight, the concealed actor leaned over from the upstairs balcony and yelled down, "Oh yeah? Well, I'm HERE tonight!"

Address 1140 Royal Street, New Orleans, LA 70116 | Hours Not open to the public; viewable from the outside only | Tip Though Nicolas Cage lost the LaLaurie mansion to foreclosure in 2009, his home for eternity remains in New Orleans. His burial site can be found in St. Louis Cemetery No. 1. Though his name is not on the tomb, the bright white stone pyramid is easy to spot.

57 Langlois Culinary Crossroads

If you can't stand the humidity, get into the kitchen

Food is New Orleans' raison d'être. Those looking to go beyond gorging at any number of the city's 1400 restaurants can gain a deeper appreciation of local specialties by taking cooking classes and learning how to prepare classic dishes like oysters Rockefeller, gumbo, and bread pudding.

Langlois Culinary Crossroads culinary school, located in a former Sicilian market, was founded by chef Amy Cirex-Sins in 2013. The name comes from Madame Langlois, the cook for a former Louisiana governor, who is considered the first Creole chef. Amy is herself an award-winning cookbook author and local radio host.

Langlois' hands-on classes are limited to 20 participants so everyone gets plenty of individualized pot-side coaching. Recent sessions have featured the making of dishes such as chicken Creole with creamed-collard-greens-stuffed crepes, jambalaya garnished with chicken cracklin', and boudin cakes made from chicken liver, rice, and a generous amount of Creole spice. Many ingredients come straight from the Langlois Crossroads Farm, located in a formerly vacant lot in the Ninth Ward.

Amy characterizes the vibe as "part cooking school, part chef's tasting table." Others have described the affordable classes as "spontaneous dinner part[ies] where anything can happen." The teaching style fervently embraces the spirit of *chacun à son goût* ("to each their own"). So whether you prefer actively mixing ingredients and getting your hands dirty or standing to the side and scribbling copious notes, you can do as you most please.

Travel & Leisure included Langlois in their article, "Best Cooking Schools Around the World," placing it alongside Le Cordon Bleu, Castello di Vicarello in Tuscany, and Two Bordelais in Bordeaux.

Address 1710 Pauger Street, New Orleans, LA 70116, +1 504.934.1010, www.langloisnola.com | **Hours** Class schedules vary; visit website to view calendar and make online reservations | **Tip** In addition to cooking classes, New Orleans offers a variety of culinary tours, on which you'll visit noted and historic restaurants to sample signature dishes. One of the more unique is a tasting tour by bike offered at Confederacy of Cruisers (www.confederacyofcruisers.com/new-orleans-culinary-bike-tour).

58__Le Musée de f.p.c.

The untold history of free people of color

Located in a Greek Revival–style house in Tremé, Le Musée de f.p.c. is a museum dedicated to black history, yet it is not a generalized African-American museum, and it only passingly has to do with slavery. Rather, the museum – one of the only institutions of its kind – is solely focused on sharing the largely unknown and fascinating tale of people of color who were born free or set free before the Civil War.

Founders Dr. Dwight and Beverly McKenna spent more than three decades collecting numerous documents, works of art, artifacts, and objects that together span 300 years of New Orleans history, dating back to 1708, when the first black Africans – two slaves named George and Marie – arrived in the city with Montreal Frenchman Jean-Baptiste Le Moyne, Sieur de Bienville, recognized as the "Father" of New Orleans.

Throughout the exhibition rooms are paintings, sculptures, and photographs by and about free people of color (f.p.c. for short) – including the lithographs of Jules Lion. Few remember Lion. He was the first African-American photographer, opening his daguerreotype studio in New Orleans in 1840, just a single year after the invention of the process. There is also ephemera such as an 1860 copy of the Dred Scott decision – from the landmark Supreme Court case – which stated that African Americans, whether free or enslaved, could not become U.S. citizens; and *Les Cenelles*, a 210-page book of poems, published in the 1840s, written by 17 free people of color.

The museum is filled with the stories of men and women from all walks of life – from tradesmen and laborers to doctors and scientists, such as the New Orleans-born chemical engineer Norbert Rillieux, who revolutionized sugar processing with his invention of a new kind of evaporator.

Le Musée offers guided tours, sponsors lectures and musical events, and on occasion presents historical reenactments with actors.

Address 2336 Esplanade Avenue, New Orleans, LA 70119, +1 504.914.5401, www.lemuseedefpc.com | **Hours** Sat and Sun noon–4:30pm or by appointment | **Tip** If you look up when entering *Le Musée*, you'll notice that the ceilings of both the first- and second-floor porches (or galleries) are painted light blue. This is a tradition common throughout the South. "Haint blue" was supposedly intended to keep away "haints," which are restless spirits of the dead who have not moved on.

Le Musée de f.p.c.
2336 Esplanade Avenue

LE MUSEE DE F.P.C. IS A HISTORIC HOUSE MUSEUM DEDICATED TO PRESERVING AND INTERPRETING THE CULTURE OF FREE PEOPLE OF COLOR IN NEW ORLEANS AND LOUISIANA DATING BACK TO THEIR PRESENCE FIRST DOCUMENTED HERE IN 1722. THE HOUSE OF CLASSIC GREEK ITALIANATE STYLE WAS BUILT IN 1859 BY DEVELOPER BENJAMIN RODRIGUEZ, WHO ALSO BUILT THE HOUSE AT 2306 ESPLANADE AVENUE, THE HOME OF RELATIVES OF EDGAR DEGAS, THE ARTIST. AND WHILE THERE IS NO RECORD OF PEOPLE OF COLOR EVER HAVING OWNED THIS HOUSE PRIOR TO THE PRESENT ONES, BECAUSE OF THEIR DOMINANCE IN THE BUILDING TRADES AND CRAFTS, THEY LIKELY CONTRIBUTED TO ITS CONSTRUCTION.

AFRO-NEW ORLEANIANS HAVE HAD AN IMPACTFUL PRESENCE IN ALL OF NEW ORLEANS. THEIR CONTRIBUTIONS ARE OF IMMENSE HISTORICAL SIGNIFICANCE TO THE VIBRANCY, ARCHITECTURAL UNIQUENESS AND BEAUTY OF THE CITY, BUT ESPECIALLY IN THIS NEIGHBORHOOD. HERE THEY TOUCHED EVERY SPHERE OF ENDEAVOR. ALONG WITH THE BUILDING TRADES, THEY INFLUENCED MUSIC, THE CULINARY ARTS, HEALTH CARE, EDUCATION, DECORATIVE ARTS, POLITICS, PUBLISHING AND RELIGION. PUBLIC RECORDS REFLECT THAT BLACKS HAVE OWNED 80 PERCENT OF THE PROPERTY IN THE AREA BOUNDED BY RAMPART STREET, ST. BERNARD AVENUE, BROAD STREET AND ORLEANS AVENUE DATING BACK TO THE SPANISH COLONIAL DAYS IN THE LATE 18TH CENTURY.

59 Le Pavillon Hotel

Come for the ghosts, stay for the PB&J

Built in 1907, Le Pavillon Hotel is nicknamed the "Belle of New Orleans." Its interior is graced with crystal chandeliers from Czechoslovakia and French marble floors and railings, imported from the lobby of the Parisian Grand Hotel; spectacular carved Italian columns and 12-foot statues frame the front entrance.

The hotel has two charming repasts; the well-attended Sunday-morning brunch in the Crystal Room and the less known nightly serving of peanut-butter-and-jelly sandwiches with milk or hot chocolate in the lobby at 10pm. The latter tradition began when a guest checked in late one evening and ordered a glass of milk at the bar. When the bartender asked about the atypical request, the guest explained that he traveled frequently and it reminded him of his daughter, whose favorite bedtime treat was always milk and a PB&J sandwich. The bartender that night happened to be the hotel's general manager, and he used his sway with the kitchen to have them whip up a plate of the classic American sandwich. They've been doing so ever since.

Like any good New Orleans hotel, Le Pavillon is also haunted. A paranormal investigation group found so much activity inside the hotel, they concluded it must be a portal to the "other side." There are regular sightings of an aristocratic middle-aged couple holding hands and walking slowly into the elevators on the second and third floors. Even after they disappear, the smell of the man's cigar lingers in the air.

If you happen to have extremely deep pockets, request Palace Suite 730 – not for the ghosts, but for the bathtub, a gift from Napoleon Bonaparte. The tub is carved from a single piece of marble. It's one of only three of its kind in the world. One sits in the Louvre. Another is in a private collection. The third is ready to receive you and your exfoliating loofah in Room 730.

Address 833 Poydras Street, New Orleans, LA 70112, +1 504.581.3111, www.lepavillon.com | Tip If you seek to round robin a series of stays at haunted hotels, other noted spots are the Hotel Monteleone (214 Royal St), which has more than a dozen guests who've yet to "check out," and the Bourbon Orleans (717 Orleans St), where you may catch sight of the famous Lady in Red.

60 Le Petit Théâtre du Vieux Carré

The little theater with the longest run

Le Petit Théâtre du Vieux Carré began in 1916 as the New Orleans chapter of the Drama League of America. At first it was a group of theater lovers who put on plays in one another's drawing rooms – primarily that of league member Mrs. Goldberg. When "serious" Irish playwright, Edward John Moreton Drax Plunkett, 18th Baron of Dunsany (he was also the chess and pistol-shooting champion of Ireland), visited New Orleans in 1922, he galvanized local thespians to get more serious about their art. The chapter bought the property at the corner of St. Peter and Chartres Streets for Le Petit Théâtre, which soon became the premier place to see live theater in the South. Over the next 95 years, Le Petit was recognized as one of the leading community playhouses in the nation.

In 2009, facing severe financial difficulties, the "Little Theater" started to unravel. First, the board of governors laid off the artistic director and staff, and then, in 2010, they announced the cancellation of the rest of the season. Enter Dickie Brennan of the Brennan restaurant empire, who felt the city must not allow its signature theater to disappear. He made a deal to buy 60 percent of Le Petit's building for a reported $3 million to establish an on-site restaurant, which allowed the theater to pay off past debts and create a sizeable endowment. The theater and the restaurant then underwent a multi-million-dollar renovation.

An upgraded theater space with new dressing rooms, offices, rehearsal rooms, lavatories, and even a new ticketing system, along with Brennan's adjacent restaurant, Tableau, were all in place when Le Petit reopened with much fanfare and community support in 2013. With an eye toward the future, the theater also launched an educational outreach program to foster the performance arts among local youth.

Address 616 St. Peter Street, New Orleans, LA 70116, +1 504.522.2081, www.lepetittheatre.com | **Hours** For tickets and performance schedule, visit the theater's website | **Tip** With the recent restoration and reopening of the two other historic theaters – the Joy Theater (1200 Canal St) and the Saenger Theatre (1111 Canal St) – there is the dream (if not quite the plan) of recreating a theatrical sector in New Orleans along Canal Street, to become "Broadway South."

61 Little Gem Saloon

A "new" jazz club with a 100-year history

Bourbon Street each night is a barrage of live music. Sadly, it's mostly bad cover bands performing Journey and Foreigner. Frenchmen Street is the better choice, where clubs, lined up one after another for two and a half blocks, feature many of the city's best musicians. Standing alone and not yet a part of a music district, there's the Little Gem Saloon.

Little Gem is located in an area that was known as Back O'Town in the early 1900s, a sketchy neighborhood bordering Storyville that experts consider the birthplace of jazz. Little Gem opened in 1903 as a dinner jazz club under the ownership of mogul Frank Doroux. He also owned the Eagle Saloon, practically next door. Many of the city's greatest jazz musicians got their starts playing at his two venues. The Iroquois Theater opened on the same block in 1911. The theater's vaudeville performances, loaded with sexual double entendres, were considered too risqué for Uptown audiences. A boyish Louie Armstrong once won a talent contest at the Iroquois for his singing and dancing.

But then, in the 1920s, two major changes dried up the neighborhood. The Federal government shut down legalized prostitution, bringing an end to Storyville; and an explosion of movie houses on Canal Street syphoned off customers from the vaudeville and jazz clubs, the last of which closed in 1927. Little Gem became a loan office. Much of the Back O'Town area was demolished to build a truly hideous-looking city hall.

More than 100 years after Little Gem opened, Dr. Nicholas Bazan and his family bought the abandoned building in 2012 and set out to restore the venue. Little Gem today is once again a popular dinner jazz club serving very good regional food and offering a lineup of outstanding musicians on its intimate stage. Regulars have included Kermit Ruffins, Meschiya Lake, Nayo Jones, and the Messy Cookers.

Address 445 Rampart Street, New Orleans, LA 70112, +1 504.267.4863, www.littlegemsaloon.com | Hours Tue–Fri 11am–10pm, Sat 5pm–11pm, Sun 10am–2pm | Tip Another noted jazz dinner club is Palm Court (1204 Decatur St). Their in-house orchestra is filled with venerable musicians. Headliner Lionel Ferbos, who died in 2014 at the age of 103, played cornet with the band until the week before his passing. But, as Palm Court is quick to point out, they "still have two 90-year-olds in the band."

62 Louis Armstrong Park
300 years of rhythm

No other location in New Orleans has more musical history or importance than Louis Armstrong Park. Within the park is Congo Square, which has been an open plaza since the city's founding, in 1718. After an expanded version of the Code Noir was approved by Louis XV in 1724, slaves in New Orleans were freed from work on Sundays and permitted to gather and socialize, which enabled them to keep their African traditions alive through music, song, and dance. They congregated each week at Congo Square to play drums and *banzas* while locals danced the traditional Calinda and juba. Arguably the physical birthplace of jazz, Congo Square saw the development of rhythms that are still heard today, not only in jazz clubs, but in second lines and Mardi Gras Indian parades.

The park itself has a long and agitated history. The ugliness began way back in 1893, when civic leaders rechristened the square, burying its African heritage by naming it after P. G. T. Beauregard, New Orleans' only Confederate general. (The name "Congo Square" wasn't officially restored until 2011). But the real mire started after legendary jazz artist and favorite son Louis Armstrong passed away, in 1971. A citizens' committee formed to discuss plans for a permanent tribute. Disagreements arose between those who wanted to draw in tourists' dollars versus those who favored enriching the lives of locals. The city dismissed several design proposals for the park as too "Disneyfied." Architect Robin Riley eventually won the job. He created a meditative park on 32 acres, which includes statues of jazz greats. The Louis Armstrong statue was sculpted by artist Elizabeth Catlett.

Louis Armstrong Park finally opened in 1980. Today, it hosts Jazz in the Park, a free weekly live music event in the spring and fall, and the annual Tremé Creole Gumbo Festival, celebrating the two things New Orleans does best: music and food.

Address 835 N Rampart Street, New Orleans, LA 70116 | Hours Daily 8am–6pm | Tip Two blocks from the park is St. Louis Cemetery No. 1, the oldest aboveground cemetery in New Orleans (1789). Marie Laveau, the famous Voodoo queen, is buried there. After a decree by the Roman Catholic archdiocese in 2015, you can only enter the cemetery with a tour guide.

63 Magnolia Bridge
A bridge over befuddled waters

Voodoo, an ancient faith rooted in spirit and ancestor worship, is practiced with great seriousness in the Crescent City. Voodoo was introduced to New Orleans in 1719 when the first African slaves arrived and brought their native languages and religious beliefs with them. The majority of enslaved Africans came from what is now the republic of Benin, in West Africa. In Benin's language, *vodun* means "spirit," an invisible, mysterious force that can intervene in human affairs.

Some of the things we now associate with the basic tenets of Voodoo, such as Voodoo queens, evolved in New Orleans. Marie Laveau is far and away the most famous Voodoo queen, but she was not the first. Sanite Dede was an earlier practitioner. She would hold ceremonies in her courtyard just blocks away from the St. Louis Cathedral. Annoyed by hearing drumbeats during their masses and outraged by rumored orgies, the church pushed through an ordinance in 1817 that decreed slaves could only dance in public on Sundays in Congo Square (see p. 132). So practitioners moved outside the then city limits to swampland on Bayou St. John, near what is now City Park. Annual rituals were performed at dusk on St. John's Eve, June 23, the most sacred of Voodoo holy days. Hundreds attended, with drums beating, bonfires, animal sacrifices, and nude women dancing seductively.

Except for the nude dancing, animal sacrifices, and bonfires (basically, just the drumming remains), a version of this yearly tradition still takes place. On Magnolia Pedestrian Bridge every June 23, people gather wearing all white for the head-washing ceremony, a form of Voodoo baptism. On the other 364 days of the year, the bridge makes for a nice picnic spot, from where you can view the Pitot House, the rotunda of Our Lady of the Holy Rosary Church, and the canoes and kayaks paddling by.

Address Corner of Moss and Harding Streets on Bayou St. John, New Orleans, LA 70119 | **Tip** Sitting on the Magnolia Bridge, you are a 10-minute walk (toward the lake) to the statue of General P. G. T. Beauregard at Esplanade and City Park Aves. Beauregard was New Orleans' only Civil War general, who virtually started the war when he fired on Ft. Sumter. Ten minutes in the other direction (toward the river) is Parkway Bakery (538 Hagan Ave), which, most years, takes Best Po'boy at the annual Po'boy Festival on Oak Street.

64 Magnolia Lane Plantation
Steeped in history and hauntings

Many visitors to New Orleans will spend the $60 (or more) to travel more than an hour each way to tour area plantations. Oak Alley is the most visited plantation on the planet and has been the setting of more than 40 movies – and Beyoncé videos. Nearby Laura Plantation has a much richer history, with its original slave quarters still intact. Magnolia Lane Plantation is a mere 20 minutes from the French Quarter and dates back to the 1830s. The dramatic grounds have been used as a location in many films, including *Bad Lieutenant: Port of Call New Orleans* and *Twelve Years a Slave*.

Magnolia Lane is a virtual amusement park of the creepy and paranormal. TV shows *Ghost Hunters*, *Ghost Adventures*, and *Scariest Places on Earth* have all filmed segments there. The property has a hanging tree where, depending on who owned the plantation at the time, both Yankees and rebel troops were strung up during the Civil War. The original owner, begging Northern soldiers not to damage his home, was shot to death on the spot and buried in a shallow grave in the front yard. Voodoo artifacts have been discovered on the plantation, an indication that the slaves of Magnolia Lane cast evil spells on their oppressive masters.

In the yard, a tree is draped with a collection of empty glass bottles hung to capture evil spirits and keep them away from the house. You can find such "bottle trees" throughout the South. Cobalt-blue vessels are the most desired, the brilliant color supposedly a better lure for spirits.

Most curious of all, in the main house there is a room dubbed the "Dying Room." Many of Magnolia's residents passed away in this room under mysterious circumstances. When asked if he's ever had experiences with ghosts, owner Richard Naberschnig replied with stories of frequent noises and furniture being moved around with no greater drama than if he'd been asked, "Have you ever eaten pizza?"

Address 2141 River Road, Nine Mile Point, LA 70094, +1 504.436.4915 | **Hours** Though the plantation is not set up for public viewing at this time, private tours may be possible by contacting the owner. | **Tip** While almost two hours outside New Orleans, Myrtles Plantation (7747 US-61, St. Francisville, LA 70775) might draw your interest as a haunted plantation where you can spend the night. The story goes that the hauntings began in the early 1800s when the owners of a slave girl, Chloe, punished her for eavesdropping by cutting her ear off. Seeking revenge, she baked a poisoned cake that killed the wife and two children of the family. Chloe was hanged from a tree, and her ghost, among others, has been spotted numerous times since.

65 Marigny Opera House
Ballet slippers and Beyoncé's sister

The former Holy Trinity Catholic Church, built in 1853, stood vacant and decaying way past "faded splendor" for fourteen years until Dave Hurlbert and partner Scott King saw a For Sale sign stuck in the front yard in 2011. When they purchased the historic edifice, Hurlbert's original intention was to turn it into a workspace. Their plans got much bigger as it grew into a "church for the arts," under-went extensive renovations (close to a million dollars' worth so far), became a nonprofit, and was rechristened the Marigny Opera House.

In its first year alone, the 160-year-old building offered an impressive number of events; it was the setting for two operas, six dance performances, two stage plays, numerous film screenings, and puppet performance art, plus three concerts and six recitals. Today, it also serves as a spiritual and community resource, hosting 12-step meetings, Sunday Musical Meditations, and gatherings of neighborhood and charitable organizations. The opera house has a resident contemporary ballet company comprising six principal dancers, who perform to live music and often debut new works such as the world premier of *Orfeo* in 2015, a ballet choreographed to an original score by local composer Tucker Fuller.

More famously, the interior – which looks like an archeological discovery, with its high vaulted ceiling, curved archways, and antique lanterns hanging a good 15 feet in the air – was the site of Depeche Mode's "Heaven" video and Solange Knowles and music-video director Alan Ferguson's highly untraditional nuptials. The entire wedding party, which included the bride's sister Beyoncé and her husband, Jay-Z, wore all white. Musicians Kelela, Questlove, and Kindness performed, and Solange and Daniel Julez, her 10-year-old son from a previous marriage, had a dance-off to the song "No Flex Zone" by the hip-hop group Rae Sremmurd.

Address 725 St. Ferdinand Street, New Orleans, LA 70117, +1 504.948.9998,
www.marignyoperahouse.org | Hours For the current performance and event schedule visit
www.marignyoperahouse.org/calendar | Tip To feed the stomach as well as the soul,
Cake Cafe & Bakery (2440 Chartres St) is a mere five blocks away. Owner Steve
Himelfarb developed a strong following selling his chocolate cake door-to-door before
opening a permanent location. During Mardi Gras season, Cake Cafe is known for their
signature king cake with apple-and-goat-cheese filling.

66__Meyer the Hatter

Where "old hat" is a compliment

At some point, whether it was Brad Pitt styling a beat-up porkpie in *Snatch* or Michael Jackson flipping a fedora in the *Billie Jean* music video, men's hats became fashionable again. Mail-order catalogs and brick-and-mortar hat stores began cropping up everywhere. Meyer the Hatter had been there all along. Opened in 1894, it is both the oldest and the largest hat store in the South.

Paul, the great-grandson of the original owner, runs the shop today. He took over the business when his dad, Mister Sam, turned 80 years old. Now more than 90, Mister Sam still comes to work every day – he's been a fixture at Meyer the Hatter since 1946. "I wasn't brought up to chase balls on a golf course or putter in the garden," he explains. He married Marcelle in 1959 and thereafter she too has been an everyday presence. Paul's brother and two sons also work at the store. The result is a shop filled with family banter and congenial complaining.

Hats are everywhere: stacked three and four high on counters, dangling from random hooks, resting on glass shelves, and tucked inside the many towers of shipping cartons that clog the long, narrow aisles. Straw hats from Ecuador are joined by berets from France, bowlers from England, an Italian straw boater if you want to look like a gondolier, or the yet-to-be-sold cherry-red beaver-fur homburg.

Prices are reasonable, generally between $75 and $250, and the service is – as to be expected in a 120-year-old-family business – exceptional. The Meyer clan will give you lessons in hat etiquette (don't pinch a hat) and expert advice on what style fits your face.

With their reputation and vast inventory, it is not surprising that Meyer the Hatter is the go-to store in New Orleans for costume designers in search of the perfect topper to complete a film character's look. Notes Mister Sam, "You don't look at John Wayne's shoes."

Address 120 St. Charles Avenue, New Orleans, LA 70130, +1.504.525.1048, www.meyerthehatter.com | **Hours** Mon–Sat 10am–5:45pm | **Tip** More movies are made in New Orleans each year (usually 90 to 100) than anywhere else in the United States. Keep an eye out for the Day-Glo signs posted all over town that point film crews to current shooting locations.

67 __ Milton Latter Library

A luxury library for leisurely learning

Many visitors, and more than a few locals, want to take tours of the large antebellum mansions which dot the Garden District and line St. Charles Avenue. A few open their doors for Spring Home & Garden tours, but the private homes are generally off-limits.

The Milton Latter Library, perhaps the most elegant library on the planet, is a grand exception. During their opening hours, anyone can walk in and stay as long as they like (until closing). You can browse the paper, read a book, or just rest awhile in one the various parlors' ornate velvet chairs.

The beaux-arts mansion occupies an entire block. The house sits loftily atop a sloping landscape, looking down on the neighborhood and the St. Charles streetcar line. It was designed by architects Favrot and Livaudais for department store owner Mark Isaacs, and built in 1907.

Inside the house, you'll be dazzled by the chandeliers and mirrors imported from Czechoslovakia, massive dining-room mantels, Dutch murals with German mottoes, and carved Flemish-style woodwork. Most immediately impressive is the sweeping 25-step staircase that looks like Sunset Boulevard's Norma Desmond might descend at any moment, ready for her close-up. This is totally appropriate, as it was for years the home of silent-film star Marguerite Clark. Marguerite was one of New Orleans' first glamorous celebrities-in-residence, a good 75 years before Brad Pitt or Sandra Bullock. Her portrait rests at the landing of the staircase.

The last private owners of the home were Mr. and Mrs. Harry Latter. They bought the house in 1947 for $100,000, not to live there, but to create a memorial to their son Milton, who had been killed in the Battle of Okinawa. They spent $25,000 converting the estate into a luxurious library, which they donated to the city of New Orleans. Milton's portrait still hangs proudly in the foyer.

Address 5120 St. Charles Avenue, New Orleans, LA 70115, +1 504.596.2625 |
Hours Mon–Fri 9am–6pm, Sat–Sun, noon–5pm | Tip The Women's Opera Guild
(2504 Prytania St) is the one residence in the Garden District that does (sometimes) offer
tours. The Greek Revival house was built in 1865. It can be seen by appointment on certain
Mondays only and is a quick stop on Gray Line's Garden District tour.

68 Miss Claudia's

Stylish home of "ain't there no mo'"

Step inside Miss Claudia's Vintage Clothing & Costumes and your senses will instantly be assaulted by decades of eclectic vintage pieces: 1920s beaded sheath dresses, 1940s men's silk smoking jackets, 1960s go-go dresses, 1970s powder-blue leisure suits, 1980s poufy-sleeved pastel prom gowns (were those ever right?). Owned by local actor and singer Claudia Baumgarten, Miss Claudia's is the oldest non-corporate vintage and costume shop in New Orleans run by a sole proprietor. While her shop primarily carries Southern vintage and showcases labels from local stores that "ain't there no mo'," such as D. H. Holmes and Maison Blanche, the store is receptive of all things vintage and all things fun. Digging through her clothing racks, you are likely to find everything from velvet opera capes to old lettermen jackets, to a 1950s sheer pink lace pleated tulle party dress that harks back to Grace Kelly.

After Hurricane Katrina, so many new grassroots krewes sprang up to celebrate New Orleans culture that Baumgarten expanded her costume selection. While it's typical of many New Orleanians to have a "costume closet," you don't need to have an entire space dedicated to the art of dressing up to be able to find room for a few vibrantly colored wigs, some rhinestone jewelry, glittery platform boots, colorful tights and tutus, or unusual collectible cuff links. Aside from costuming for Halloween and Mardi Gras, you can also pick up a flowered headpiece for Day of the Dead, lederhosen for Oktoberfest, or a green top hat for St. Patrick's Day. And if you're unsure exactly what look you're striving for, bring in your ideas, and the staff, who "specialize in imagination," will help you put together the perfect ensemble.

Baumgarten says that her clientele ranges from the bohemian to the conservative, proof that costuming in New Orleans is truly egalitarian.

Address 4204 Magazine Street, New Orleans, LA 70115, +1 504.897.6310, www.missclaudias.com | **Hours** Mon–Fri 10am–6pm, Sat 10am–6pm, Sun noon–5pm | **Tip** When you're finished at Miss Claudia's, stroll down to the Club Ms. Mae's (4336 Magazine St). It takes pride in being New Orleans' cheapest 24-hour dive bar. In 2011, well drink prices were finally adjusted for inflation, going from $1 to $2. New Orleanians, not the best with change, did not protest and accepted the "rate hike" with a raised glass.

69___Modern Gargoyles

Things are looking up

If you look aloft at certain locations in the city you might spot some particularly grotesque gargoyles clinging to the sides of buildings, holding their victims' torn-off heads. These are the work of Randy Morrison, a noted Mardi Gras float sculptor who has recently turned his creativity toward making and propagating these macabre outdoor figures. The creatures are constructed of lightweight steel-reinforced fiberglass foam, each gargoyle weighing about 15 pounds.

Medieval churches, especially in France, were adorned with gargoyles possibly for two conflicting reasons. One was to scare evil spirits away. The other was to illustrate what horrors awaited the townsfolk if they didn't get their butts into the pews and load up the collection plates. Their functional purpose was as gutter spouts to direct rainwater off the roofs.

A complete history of gargoyles was lavished, nearly relentlessly, upon Morrison by his neighbor, Gregory Lewis, in an effort to persuade him to create a gargoyle for the exterior of his house. Finally won over (or worn down), Morrison worked by night for several months in a spider-infested shop owned by Lewis to sculpt the beast.

Lewis mounted the gargoyle on Halloween 2012. The statue was an immediate success, as evidenced by the number of strangers who subsequently solicited Morrison to make gargoyles for their homes or businesses, including a former synagogue at 709 Jackson Street – where, as soon as the ghoulish sculpture was installed, the frequent incidents of neighborhood kids breaking windows in the vacant building mysteriously ceased. Morrison's gargoyles are now in several states and three locations around the city. In the patter of tour guides on the Hop On Hop Off buses, Morrison has been amused to overhear some say that his gargoyles were placed on houses to ward off evil during the yellow fever outbreaks in the late 19th century.

Address 1469 Magazine Street, 1507 Magazine Street (St. Vincent's Guest House), and 709 Jackson Avenue, New Orleans, LA 70130 | Tip Alex Podesta is sometimes called the bunny-man artist. His life-sized statues of grown, bearded men in bunny outfits peer down from the rooftop of 1228 Oretha Castle Haley Blvd. Each one was sculpted using a plaster mask of Podesta's own face.

70__Musée Conti Wax Museum
Wax on, wax off, wax hanging on by a thread

Making lifelike figures in wax goes back at least to the Middle Ages, when a funeral for a royal or a priest entailed carrying the corpse on top of the coffin. In really hot weather, this resulted in stomach-turning consequences; so instead, wax effigies were made to travel from church to gravesite.

In 1835, Madame Tussaud established the world's first commercial wax museum, on Baker Street in London. Here patrons could gawk at celebrities like Voltaire, opera star Maria Malibran, and various kings and popes. By the late 19th century, the wax-museum craze had taken hold and most large cities had one. In recent decades, many wax museums have met their demise, unable to compete with glitzier, more technologically enhanced forms of entertainment.

Musée Conti Wax Museum, which opened in New Orleans in 1963, remains a disheveled but delightful artifact of a bygone era. Most of the figures were made in France, using imported hairs from Italy and glass eyeballs from Germany. While other wax museums showcase celebrity likenesses, the Musée Conti is devoted to the 300-year history of New Orleans (including a mandatory Haunted Dungeon).

More than 150 life-sized figures tell the story of the Big Easy, including Iberville and Bienville laying claim to the "Accidental City" in a swamp, Napoleon sitting in a bathtub arguing over the sale of Louisiana, the pirate Jean Lafitte, Andrew Jackson at the Battle of New Orleans, Marie Laveau surrounded by Voodoo dancers, a Mardi Gras Zulu King, and iconic musician Louis Armstrong.

Some visitors complain about the musty smell, poor lighting, and statues in need of a tune up. Musée Conti is, like other wax museums, hanging on by a thread. But for the cognoscenti, the state of disrepair is added appeal. The Dracula on display needs to bite into his victim soon – her 50-year-old wax head is about to fall off from age and inattention.

Address 917 Conti Street, New Orleans, LA 70112, +1(504) 525-2605, www.neworleanswaxmuseum.com | **Hours** Mon, Fri, and Sat 10am–4pm | **Tip** The spirits of Andrew Jackson and pirate Jean Lafitte can also be found at Pierre Maspero's restaurant (440 Chartres St). The two are rumored to have once met there to plan the Battle of New Orleans. The British had solicited Lafitte to help them navigate the waterways from the Gulf of Mexico to launch an attack on New Orleans for control of the Mississippi. Lafitte met with Jackson to entertain a better offer. Given the promise of his brother's release from jail, Lafitte signed over his 1000 men, who proved critical in defeating the British.

71 Museum of Death
Morbid menagerie

If the Torture Museum in Amsterdam or the Akodessewa Fetish Market in Lomé, Togo, seem too far to travel, New Orleans' Museum of Death just joined the ranks of the macabre in 2015.

The original Museum of Death started in San Diego in 1995 in a building once owned by Wyatt Earp, then moved to Los Angeles after they were evicted for bringing unwanted publicity to the landlord when they tried to acquire enough artifacts from the Heaven's Gate cult suicides to recreate the death scene in its entirety.

The new New Orleans location, which owner J. D. Healy calls "a work in progress" has a DIY, Mr. Ferguson's barn feeling to it. Once you've proved you can stomach the "tester" exhibits in the entryway (a human skull and teeth, a goat head, and a gory depiction of a freeway accident) and heed the ticket taker's warning – "It's pretty graphic back there" – you pass through a makeshift curtained entrance into the exhibition rooms.

There, you'll find a grisly collection of death-related items: bizarre drawings and letters by mass murderers, an assortment of death-row shanks; skulls; bottled fetuses; a clearly posed taxidermy snake claimed to be "eating itself"; a Ripley's-Believe-It-or-Not-like fur-covered fish; a death mask of Adolf Hitler that's clearly been dropped, as evidenced by the broken-off nose; and a bra and panties worn by serial killer Aileen Wuornos. There are also some not-for-kids crime-scene photos, an autopsy video, and a screening room playing film loops of people dying in public.

The museum feels like a throwback to the days of exotic sideshows and carnival freak tents. Up front there is a gift shop selling T-shirts, hoodies, coffee mugs, and the most desirable item, the Serial Killer Trivia Game.

Special note: if you faint in the Museum of Death, you get a free T-shirt.

Address 227 Dauphine Street, New Orleans, LA 70112, +1 504.593.3968, www.museumofdeath.net | Hours Wed–Mon 10am–6pm | Tip A five-block walk will take you to a truly morbid spot, the St. Peter Guest House (1005 St Peter St). Here, in Room 37, Johnny Thunders, guitar player in the New York Dolls, was found dead, allegedly from a drug overdose – his body twisted and stiff from rigor mortis. Despite the fact that the room had been ransacked, a criminal investigation was never opened. There's often a six–month waiting list for Room 37.

72 _ Musicians' Village
Restoring the groove

When visitors come to New Orleans and want to see the "Katrina area," they usually mean the Lower Ninth Ward and the Make It Right homes funded by, among others, Brad Pitt (to the tune of $6 million). Since 2005, Musicians' Village, located in the Upper Ninth Ward, has played the backup role, or the "other" place to witness New Orleans' rebirth.

The idea for Musicians' Village came when Harry Connick, Jr. and Branford Marsalis returned to their city weeks after the storm and were overwhelmed by the restoration work that needed to be done. The two teamed up with Habitat for Humanity and partnered with an existing home-building project, the Baptist Crossroads, to create a new neighborhood, a village for New Orleans musicians who lost their homes in the flood. The community now comprises 72 houses, all built over 5.5 feet off the ground, or a foot above the flood level in the area. The houses are very modestly priced, barely above construction costs, and each homeowner is responsible for paying off the interest-free mortgage.

The centerpiece of Musicians' Village is the Ellis Marsalis Center for Music, which is dedicated to celebrating and supporting the musicians of New Orleans and to the music education of the next generation. The 17,000-square-foot facility features a 170-seat theater as well as practice rooms, recording booths, classrooms, and a community computer room and listening library. An after-school arts program for students aged 7 to 18 focuses on teaching the fundamentals of instrumental music, dance, and music theory. Professional musicians provide instruction for the incredibly low cost of $30 per term.

Since the center opened, in 2011, they've hosted a Tuesday-night concert series where patrons can enjoy live performances by such noted musicians as Shamarr Allen, Mark Braud, and Bob French's Original Tuxedo Band for a mere $3.

THE ELLIS MARSALIS CENTER FOR MUSIC

New Orleans Habitat

Musicians' Village

Address The Ellis Marsalis Center for Music, 1901 Bartholomew Street, New Orleans, LA 70117, +1 504.940.3400, www.ellismarsaliscenter.org | Hours Check website for programs and events | Tip Free concerts take place throughout New Orleans, depending on the time of the year. Lafayette Square has a 12-week series on Wednesday evenings from mid-March to mid-June and features top local musicians, like Kermit Ruffins and Irma Thomas, as well as the occasional national performer, like Buddy Guy. Congo Square's weekly Jazz in the Park series runs in the spring and the fall. It likewise features known regional performers, such as Allen Toussaint, Charmaine Neville, and Rockin Dopsie.

73__New Canal Lighthouse

Illuminating exhibits

A lighthouse has stood near this spot along the shores of Lake Pontchartrain since 1838. The first was a cypress tower topped with a lantern, which was set about 1000 feet offshore. By 1843, many of the lighthouse's timbers had begun to rot, which required a new one be built. In 1880, the Southern Yacht Club relocated from Biloxi, Mississippi, to New Orleans and their nearby building blocked the lantern's light, rendering it useless. So the old lighthouse was sold for scrap and another was constructed in 1890, this one 16 feet taller than the original. This version was damaged by hurricanes in 1903, 1915, 1926, and 1927. Hurricanes Katrina and Rita caused further destruction in 2005, leaving the lighthouse a splintered and disassembled mess.

In 2006, the Lake Pontchartrain Basin Foundation, owners of the light-house, signed a lease with the United States Coast Guard to restore it. All that could be salvaged was gathered, disassembled, and stored for re-use. The beacon was finally relit in 2012 and full reconstruction, incorporating materials from the 1890 lighthouse, was completed in 2013. Included in the modernized lighthouse is an education center, where you can take a self-guided tour to learn about the animal habitats of the Lake Pontchartrain Basin and what's being done to address critical coastal issues such as flooding and pollution.

One of the more interesting facts about the lighthouse's history is that it has had five female keepers, some who demonstrated unusual heroism in the line of duty. Caroline Riddle, who took on the post in 1895, received commendations after she secured the lantern during a powerful hurricane. Margaret Norvell is remembered for several valiant rescues. She used the station's rowboat to save a navy pilot who'd crashed his biplane into the lake. In 1925, she helped evacuate more than 200 passengers from a ferryboat that caught fire and sank near the lighthouse.

Address 8001 Lakeshore Drive, New Orleans, LA 70124, +1 504.282.2134, www.saveourlake.org | **Hours** Mon−Sat 10am−4pm | **Tip** Just down the street, NOLA Flyboarding (7400 Lakeshore Dr) is the only licensed Flyboard dealer in the state. Flyboarding is a new water sport that allows you to "fly" on jets of water to heights of up to 35 feet. Lessons are available for those over age 12 and over 80 lbs.

74__The New Movement Theater

Hoping to have the last laugh

While New Orleans is considered a hub for food and music, the same cannot yet be said for comedy. The New Movement (TNM) is a shining exception. Founders Chris Trew and Tami Nelson met in 2004 while taking classes, and before long the two crafted a dream to run their own comedy club. They felt there was enough local talent and energy that young comedians shouldn't have to run away to Chicago or New York to carve out a career.

The flood following Hurricane Katrina put their plans on hold and landed them in Austin, Texas, where they began building their New Movement empire, eventually opening a theater there and helping start partner theaters in Houston and Dallas. Finally, in 2012, they returned to NOLA and joined forces with local sketch and improv troupe Stupid Time Machine to fulfill their long-held dream: an improv school and comedy theater in their home city. Located in the Marigny, they offer classes, give workshops, and have performances throughout the week, such as the Megaphone Show, Saturday's marquee event featuring local celebrity guests. The New Movement also hosts the annual Hell Yes Fest, a two-week comedy festival.

If you attend a show, don't expect to see the typical routines and common "game-based improv," as seen on TV shows like *Whose Line Is It Anyway?* TNM espouses a wildly organic type of improv where comedians build off of one another's riffs and reactions. They also offer sketch and stand-up, and sometimes host visiting national acts.

The New Movement produced a film documenting the club's ongoing Air Sex competitions. It's like air guitar, only rather than pretending to play an invisible Fender, the performer has wild sex (thankfully fully clothed) by themselves with an utterly imaginary partner. Air Sex could well break out any night you're there.

Address 2706 St. Claude Avenue, New Orleans, LA 70117, +1 512.788.2669, www.newmovementtheater.com | **Hours** Check the performance calendar at www.newmovementtheater.com/calendar-new-orleans | **Tip** Sharing upstairs space with New Movement is Dynamo, an independent, female-run, female-friendly adult boutique. Their goal is to promote happy, healthy sexuality through education, community outreach, and high-quality, body-safe products. Dynamo's staff will also come to your home or hotel for a private Dynamo party, which offers an introduction to sex toys, as well as a basic anatomy lesson and tips for better sex.

75__New Orleans Street Gallery

Art for fresh start's sake

In March 2006, seven months after Hurricane Katrina, Jeannie and Craig Tidy returned to New Orleans and helped their daughter rebuild what was left of her flood-ravaged home. In the wake of Katrina, the city's population had dropped by nearly 60 percent. There were more than 100 destroyed properties just within a four-block radius of their daughter's house.

The Tidys did basic things like remove debris, make minor repairs, and create replacement street signs so contractors could find their way to work sites. But Jeannie's personal vision of rebuilding the city revolved around implementing a project created by Candace Lopez in San Diego, where the Tidys had relocated during the aftermath of the hurricane. In the sketchy East Village section of San Diego, unsightly gray electrical boxes could be found on practically every corner. Lopez had the idea to establish the Urban Art Trail, which involved enlisting art students to cover the traffic-signal boxes in colorful paintings, turning something unseemly and ugly into something beautiful and inspiring.

For New Orleans, Jeannie approached City Hall for the go-ahead. She was fortunate to belly up to the window of an unusually wise and generous employee who told her, "You'll never get approval in writing. But as long as the neighborhood doesn't disapprove, we won't bother you." Jeannie named the project the New Orleans Street Gallery. Artists submit an entry design for painting a utility box and, if accepted, they receive a small stipend of $250 to create the art.

The Street Gallery has since spread far beyond the initial Lakeview neighborhood into Mid-City, Carrollton, and other areas of New Orleans. So far, roughly 70 of the city's 400 utility boxes have been painted in a great variety of styles. You simply need to keep an eye out at intersections throughout the city to spot the four-sided murals.

Address At the intersection of Esplanade and Carrollton Avenues and at numerous locations throughout the city; for a list of the painted utility boxes, visit www.cvunola.org | **Tip** If you see a brightly colored statue made up of round balls that somewhat resembles a dog, that's a leftover from a benefit program to raise money for the Louisiana SPCA. The dog sculptures mimicked a well-known design kids would make from Mardi Gras beads. The statues were placed all over the city and Metairie and auctioned off.

76__NOLA Brewery
Homegrown hops with some funk

Most people mourned the closing of the Dixie Brewery following Hurricane Katrina. Instead of lamenting the loss, Kirk Coco decided to open his own brewery. Coco not only wanted New Orleans to have locally made beer to welcome people back to the city but also to create jobs. He succeeded on both counts – wildly.

NOLA Brewing launched its first two beers in 2009: NOLA Blond Ale and NOLA Brown Ale. They currently have seven year-round beers, with such New Orleans-inspired names as Hopitoulas (a play on the street where the brewery resides, Tchoupitoulas) and 7th Street Wheat (to honor the Seventh Street Wharf across the road); five seasonal beers (among others, a French Saison-style ale named Hurricane Saison); and according to Coco, "a number of beers that come out at odd times during the year."

In 2013, NOLA Brewing added taps and tables to its break room and opened it to the public, but quickly outgrew the space. They expanded to a new taproom next door that features two bars with 24 taps, including the NOLA funk series of sour beers that are named after area streets (Lowerline, a tart lemon; Arabella, a peach sour; Piety, a cherry sour; and Sauvage, a pale ale).

The taproom not only embodies the upscale but low-key personality of NOLA Brewery, it also features personalized touches – all of the tables are made from wooden barrels that once aged NOLA beer and the art is all by local artists. They offer food from McClure's BBQ, have a pop-up kitchen every Tuesday, and once a month host a special event with music and beer specials. Thankfully, even with their growth, NOLA Brewery still frequently offers a Friday-afternoon tour from 2pm to 3pm, where you can learn about the history of the brewery while enjoying free beer. While on the tour, make sure you look up – Coco stores the marching krewe Jefferson Dragons' colorful costumes in the upper portion of the brewery.

Address 3001 Tchoupitoulas Street, New Orleans, LA 70115, +1 504.896.9996, www.nolabrewing.com | Hours Taproom: 11am–11pm | Tip Although the old Falstaff brewery has been closed for more than 30 years, its locally iconic sign remains. The building is now an apartment complex, and the 11-story sign and its "weatherball" atop were recently restored. Curious about the weather forecast? If the orb is green it means fair weather; red means cloudy or overcast; flashing red means rain; and flashing red and white means storms are approaching.

77_Norma Wallace House
The best little whorehouse with class

Entering the French Quarter on Conti Street from Rampart, there's a three-story gray building with dark green shutters. Unsightly parking lots sit to its left and right. Most people drive right by the house without pause, unwittingly flying by one of the Quarter's most interesting addresses.

1026 Conti Street was once the home of posthumously famous photographer E. J. Bellocq (1873–1949). Buried in the mess of his apartment and discovered after his death were hundreds of pictures he'd taken of the prostitutes of Storyville. Subjects were partially or altogether naked except for the black masks that some wore, and many of the images had the faces of the prostitutes intentionally scratched out. Bellocq's photos have been exhibited in art museums throughout the country and can be seen in the permanent collection of the New Orleans Museum of Art.

Even more famously, or infamously, 1026 Conti is known for being Norma Wallace's establishment for 25 years. Miss Norma was the madam of an upscale brothel that catered to the wealthy, the famous, and the powerful. Wallace won the protection of the cops when she helped them capture gangster Alvin Karpis, the FBI's No. 1 most wanted. The New Orleans Police Department got the credit and the commendation from President Hoover; Norma got their undivided inattention. Still, as an insurance policy, she kept a book that listed all of her patrons. She had names, dates, and, in an era long before naked selfies, sizes and detailed descriptions of her clients' private "assets."

The building has been painstakingly restored and now houses seven apartments, each named after one of the ladies who worked there. Norma once said of her life as a madam: "I used to wake up around noon and have my coffee and wonder what this night's going to bring … It was exciting … There was never a dull moment. You can believe me when I tell you that."

Address 1026 Conti Street, New Orleans, LA 70112, www.1026contistreet.com |
Hours Not open to the public; viewable from the outside only | Tip A few doors down,
at 1017 and 1019 Conti St, are two surviving houses of the great fires of 1788 and 1794,
which destroyed 80 percent of the city. The French Quarter was largely rebuilt under
Spanish rule, using Spanish architecture. In contrast, these two earlier buildings display
the steep-pitched roofs the Cajuns had learned to use in Canada to keep snow from
piling up – a style that makes not a lick of sense in subtropical New Orleans.

78__One Eyed Jacks

A club with a twist (and some turns)

A mere half block from loud and obnoxious bars on Bourbon Street, One Eyed Jacks is an elegant throwback to another era (in a faded-splendor way). Now a music and performance space, the venue passed through several previous lives as an entertainment hub. Opened in 1970 as a movie palace, it later became the epicenter for the rebirth of burlesque in New Orleans.

In the 1960s, an overzealous DA, Jim Garrison, nearly destroyed NOLA as the burlesque capital by driving out merely risqué acts like Rita Alexander, the Champagne Girl, who balanced full glasses of bubbly on her breasts. But rather than cleansing the city of bawdy vaudevillian entertainment, Garrison created a void later filled by much raunchier live sex acts.

In the 1990s, drummer Ronnie Magri – who possessed a love of retro-kitsch burlesque, but not an ounce of knowledge – rented old B movies, interviewed retired dancers to recreate historic routines, and formed the Shim Sham Revue, New Orleans' "first burlesque revival troupe." They became a mainstay of the former movie palace, known then as the Shim Sham Club. The club provided a link between the burlesque stars of yesteryear and the modern wave of performers like Trixie Minx, Bella Blue, and troupes Fleur de Tease and Dames D'Lish.

In 2002, the club came under new ownership and reopened as One Eyed Jacks. The front bar, the original lobby, sports ornate chandeliers and gilt-framed paintings of nudes that line red-flocked damask wallpaper. The spacious main room features the stage and a large horseshoe-shaped bar. Upstairs, the balcony is a discreet lounge called the Matador, with velvet bullfighting paintings. In addition to burlesque acts, the club is known for showcasing emerging indie bands like Hurray for the Riff Raff, and deviant musicians like Quintron & Miss Pussycat. It also hosts the not-to-be-missed Bingo! Show and the ever-popular Fast Times 80s Dance Night.

Address 615 Toulouse Street, New Orleans, LA 70130, +1 504.569.8361, www.oneeyedjacks.net | Hours Mon–Wed 7pm–2am, Thu 8pm–4am, Fri and Sat 7pm–3am | Tip The New Orleans Bingo! Show started in 2002 when front man Clint Maedgen found bingo game boards in a thrift store and was inspired to create a new performance piece. The act merges theater, rock music, burlesque, comedic skits, and short films, and, in the middle of the set, everything stops while the audience plays a round of bingo. If you win, for God's sake don't tell anyone, unless you want to be dragged up onstage and utterly humiliated before getting your prize.

79__Our Mother of Perpetual Help

Home to priests, a vampire novelist, and a ghost rider

After the Louisiana Purchase, in 1803, Americans swarmed into New Orleans. There were, at the time, many ways to get stinking rich in the city: cotton, sugar, coffee, the slave trade, and anything to do with the shipping industry. The new arrivals were far from embraced by the Creole residents. Unwelcome in the French Quarter, they settled upriver in what's now known as the Garden District. Here, they built huge Greek Revival, Italianate, and Queen Anne Victorian mansions.

Choose any street in this neighborhood to view stunning ornate houses with rich histories. Prytania Street's collection includes Colonel Short's Villa, used as the Yankees' headquarters when they occupied New Orleans during the Civil War; the Women's Opera Guild, the only home in the Garden District that provides regular tours; and a mansion at 2523 Prytania Street with a beautiful front-yard chapel. The latter was designed in 1857 by celebrated architect Jacques Nicolas Bussière de Pouilly. The 13-room, 13,200-square-foot mansion includes six bedrooms, four kitchens, and an elevator. There's a 33-foot-long walk-in closet and a spa tub surrounded by Greek columns set in the center of one of the five bathrooms.

After the Civil War, the Redemptorist Fathers bought the house and converted it into a residence for older priests. They added the chapel built into the front-yard fence. The vine-covered cast-iron pavilion still has "Our Mother of Perpetual Help" in big letters topped with a large gold cross. The chapel served the parish until 1996, when the house was sold to Anne Rice. She never lived there, but her novel *Violin* is set in the house. She sold it to antiques dealer Reuban "Buzz" Harper who, in turn, sold it to actor Nicolas Cage. Cage, like Rice, once had multiple homes in New Orleans. Reportedly owing millions in back taxes, he had to sell them all.

Address 2523 Prytania Street, New Orleans, LA 70130 | Hours Not open to the public; viewable from the outside only | Tip Take a walk down nearby Coliseum St between Fourth St and Washington Ave to see a row of five identical Greek Revival houses built in 1861 by architect William Freret. They became known as Freret's Folly because the Civil War broke out as construction of the houses was nearing completion, and home values tanked, leaving Freret in the red. Hard to imagine such a history when you consider one of the homes was on the market for $2.6 million in 2014.

80__Pagoda Café
Coffee and a bike tune-up

Australian Dan Etheridge, who has a background in architecture, was drawn to the building that now houses his coffee shop because of its unusual pagoda-style roof. The location had been part of Charles Tung's Oriental Laundry chain, which was headquartered on Bourbon Street but operated from numerous spots throughout New Orleans in the 1930s. It had been vacant for years prior to being purchased by Dan and his former catering partner and cook, Shana Sassoon, a Texan by way of India.

Pagoda Café, opened in 2013, not only looks distinctly indie, but the atmosphere is fundamentally more delightfully peculiar than the half-decaf, nonfat soy frappuccino-slinging monotony of the chain coffeehouses. Whereas you can always get your gluten-free, taste-free Marshmallow Dream Bar at any of the 23,179 Starbucks, if you come back to Pagoda for one of the pressed Chisesi ham, brie, and blood-orange marmalade sandwiches you had on your last visit, you may have to "settle" for the vegetarian banh mi of beets, pickled vegetables, and an Indian-style chutney – the menu changes often. The breakfast and lunch offerings are consistently delicious, fresh, and always affordable.

More, much more, than the coffee and the food, the "happenings" at Pagoda Café are the real draw for customers, much like the Greenwich Village coffeehouses of the beat generation. On a recent Sunday, there were two fiddlers playing Appalachian folk music, an artisan baker selling bread from the back of a truck, and a pop-up bicycle repair. Pagoda also hosts after-hours reggae dance parties from 6pm to 9pm on the first Sunday of each month.

Like any good coffeehouse, there is an oversized note board with pinned flyers and business cards. Pagoda's board, however, has fewer apartment rental notices and write-your-term-paper ads and more African Helix stitch lessons and hoodoo rootwork offerings.

HOT & COLD
DRINKS
RESH FOOD
ADE DAILY"

Pagoda
Café

Address 1430 N Dorgenois Street, New Orleans, LA 70119, +1 504.644.4178,
www.pagodacafe.net | Hours Tue – Sat 7am – 4pm, Sun 9am – 3pm | Tip Pagoda Café is
situated at the intersection of Broad St and Bayou Rd, the base of the "Bayou Corridor,"
home to CoCo Hut (Jamaican takeout food), Community Book Center (a collection
of books by and about African Americans), Domino Sound (the largest selection of
reggae 45s and LPs in the South), and Club Caribbean (a reggae club featuring DJs
and biweekly live shows).

81 Piazza d'Italia

Mister Moore's neighborhood

The Warehouse District, once literally nothing but industrial warehouses, has grown to become a hub of great award-winning restaurants. Julia Street, lined with galleries, has replaced the French Quarter as New Orleans' art district. It is also "museum central," with the Ogden Art Museum, the Contemporary Art Museum, the Children's Museum, the Civil War Museum, and the massive and ever-expanding World War II Museum.

In the midst of the now thriving neighborhood is a weird city block of brightly colored but seemingly unfinished buildings and a nonfunctioning fountain in front of a nonfunctioning clock tower. The area looks like a movie set, and in fact it has been – most recently for one of the *Planet of the Apes* sequels.

It is actually the Piazza d'Italia, an award-winning tribute to the Italian immigrants of New Orleans, designed by the well-known postmodern architect Charles Moore. Moore worked collaboratively with three architects from the Perez firm in New Orleans to conceive an abstract public fountain in the shape of the Italian peninsula surrounded by multiple colonnades, a clock tower, and a Roman temple.

Completed in 1978, the Piazza d'Italia debuted to widespread acclaim. It was intended to be a "surprise plaza" like those found in Mediterranean cities, where pedestrians suddenly emerge from narrow passage ways to find an open square lined with cafes and shops. However, rapid deterioration set in because the surrounding area never blossomed. Many New Orleanians have neither seen nor ever heard of the square. Others refer to it as the first "postmodern ruin."

There are ongoing efforts to revive the plaza. In 2013, the mayor announced $280,000 in funds to help restore the Piazza d'Italia to the gathering place it was always intended to be. For now, it remains a vision of a city that seems to have sprung from the mind of Salvador Dali or Max Ernst.

Address Lafayette Street at Commerce Street, New Orleans, LA 70130 | **Tip** There is a smaller and more "normal" tribute to the Irish of New Orleans in the form of the Irish Cultural Museum (933 Conti St) in the French Quarter. Beginning in the 1700s, New Orleans received many Irish immigrants. During the Potato Famine (1845 and 1852) thousands arrived in the port city and provided cheap construction labor. Nearly 8000 died digging the New Basin Canal, which was later filled in, during the 1950s.

82 Pontalba Buildings

Apartments fit for a baroness

Jackson Square – with the famous St. Louis Cathedral at the back and the perhaps more famous Café Du Monde at the front – is the white-hot center of tourism in New Orleans. However, hiding in plain sight are some less known but more interesting stories about its history. If you look up at the long brick buildings on St. Peter and St. Ann Streets on either side of the square, you can make out the letters AP in the striking wrought-iron design along the second- and third-floor verandas. The monogram signifies the two families Almonester and Pontalba, once the wealthiest in Louisiana.

Micaela Almonester (1795–1874) was the only child of one of the oldest Creole families in New Orleans. When her father died in 1798, she became the sole heir to his fortune. Micaela was married to her cousin, Xavier Celestin Delfau de Pontalba, when she was 15. Xavier's father, the baron Joseph Delfau de Pontalba, constantly schemed (unsuccessfully) to acquire his daughter-in-law's fortune. Infuriated by her resistance, he confronted Micaela and shot her four times with a pistol. She lost two of her fingers and was maimed in the chest, but did not die. The baron, however, committed suicide.

More than a survivor, Micaela became an Oprah-like force of nature. She left Xavier and then almost single-handedly cleaned up the slum that had become the Place d'Armes at the city's center. For $300,000 she constructed the two new Parisian-style rowhouses known today as the Pontalba buildings. She then led the campaign to rename the square after Andrew Jackson, to appeal to the influx of Americans and, not coincidentally, to raise the value of her real estate.

At one point, the famous opera singer Jenny Lind stayed as a guest in one of the Pontalba apartments. Ever the entrepreneur, Micaela predated eBay by 200 years when she auctioned off everything the singing sensation had sat on or walked across.

Address 700 Decatur Street, New Orleans, LA 70116 | **Tip** In 1856, Baroness Pontalba provided funding for the square's statue of Andrew Jackson on his horse. It's little known that the artist, Clark Mills, created three more identical ones, for Washington, DC, Nashville, and Jacksonville, FL. Legend has it that New Orleans' Jackson tips his hat directly at Apartment Number 5, on the St. Peter-St side, where the Baroness Pontalba lived.

83__The Prayer Room at St. Louis Cathedral

Who dat say Henriette can't be no saint?

The St. Louis Cathedral is the oldest Catholic church in continual use in America and the most photographed and iconic architectural symbol of New Orleans. In other words, the cathedral is hardly a hidden treasure. But there are some lesser-known stories about this legendary landmark. One interesting tale involves Adrien de Pauger. He was the original designer of the cathedral. Pauger wanted to be buried under the floorboards, then considered a great honor, but he died in 1726, before the church was completed. To fulfill his wishes, workers improvised: they put Pauger's body inside a wall and just kept going.

Many of the interior decorations refer to the church's namesake, Saint Louis. Prior to sainthood, he was crowned Louis IX, king of France, when he was only 12 years old. He spent a lifetime caring for and feeding the poor, and died leading the Crusade in 1267 against the Muslims in Syria. There are 10 colorful stained-glass windows overhead that narrate his life story. A large mural above the altar shows King Louis announcing his Crusade.

But one of the more beautiful and peaceful spots in the cathedral is the not often visited Prayer Room, located near the entrance where the baptistery once was. The newer stained-glass windows depict Mother Henriette Delille, to whom the room is dedicated. Delille was a New Orleans Creole woman born around 1812 who founded the Sisters of the Holy Family, a group comprising free women of color. The order provided nursing care and a home for orphans, slaves, and the elderly, and later established schools as well.

Pope Benedict XVI approved Henriette as "venerable" in 2010. That's sort of like earning a brown belt in tae kwon do. Should she make it all the way to sainthood, she would be New Orleans' first saint and her already planned dedication would be the first on U.S. soil.

Address 615 Pere Antoine Alley, New Orleans, LA 70116, +1 504.525.9585, www.stlouiscathedral.org | Hours Daily, after the 7:30am mass–4pm | Tip Drew Brees is already a Saint, and probably the most beloved in the NFL franchise's history. His nearly 5000-square-foot home is nestled in the Audubon neighborhood. Last time the Saints won a Superbowl, fans turned his front gate into a Buddhist shrine, tying notes to the fence, and leaving him flowers and baked goods by the entrance.

84__Prytania Theatre

Where the owner is as entertaining as the films

New Orleans has a rich history of cinema. In 1896, the first movie house in the United States, Vitascope Hall, opened on Canal Street. Admission was ten cents. For an extra ten cents, you could peek into the booth to watch the projectionist, and for another dime you could buy a frame of discarded film. Imagine what those frames would be worth today.

A bit of a less historic (it opened in 1914) but honored spot is the Prytania Theatre, the oldest New Orleans movie house still in operation and the only single-screen theater remaining in Louisiana. The theater began as an outdoor venue, where patrons literally received a "rain check" if it rained. The Prytania survived a devastating fire in 1926, which allowed for elaborate improvements during the restoration, like a red-velvet-and-polished-brass lobby, a new façade, and a state-of-the-art Hillgreen-Lane organ (this was the silent film era, when the accompanying organ occupied a pivotal role).

The Prytania now shows "talkies" using Sony Digital 4K projection and Dolby Digital surround sound. They screen first-run releases and also premiere movies starring or made by New Orleanians. Every year, before the Academy Awards, they play nominated films, even obscure ones, and host an annual Oscar party.

But the absolute treasure of the Prytania is owner Rene Brunet Jr. Now in his 90s, he no longer greets every customer at the door. His son Robert has taken over that job. But Rene is easy to spot inside, with his signature suit and movie-themed tie. It's been said that after paying admission, your most entertaining evening can be spent by skipping the movie and talking to Rene instead. He is a historian of grand movie palaces and author of a book about movie theaters in New Orleans. Rene's love for the Prytania shines through. He once said about his chosen career: "I feel like I'm host to a party every day and every night."

Address 5339 Prytania Street, New Orleans, LA 70115, +1 504.891.2787, www.prytaniatheatreneworleans.com | **Hours** Check website for screening schedule | **Tip** At the opposite end of the movie-going experience are the Theatres at Canal Place (333 Canal St, 3rd floor), located in an upscale mall. Here you can watch current blockbusters from VIP plush leather motorized recliners; every one has a personal table, drink holder, and call button for in-seat food and cocktail service throughout the show.

85 — The Rebirth Statue

The game changer for an entire city

There are many statues of sports stars outside their one-time home stadiums. A bronzed Michael Jordan executes a monster dunk in front of the United Center in Chicago; the Bryant-Denny Stadium for the Alabama Crimson Tide has a full huddle of legendary football coaches. Baltimore-born Babe Ruth stands by the Orioles ballpark (even though he actually never played for them). But none elicits a greater emotional response than the statue of New Orleans Saints player Steve Gleason blocking a punt by an Atlanta Falcon, outside the Superdome.

The actual play occurred September 25, 2006, at the beginning of a Monday Night NFL game. The match-up against the Falcons marked the Saints' official return to their stadium, a year after Hurricane Katrina all but shut the city down and sent the Saints to San Antonio, Baton Rouge, and New York City for their 2005 "home" games.

The blocked punt was recovered for a touchdown and set off a roar described as "nothing anyone heard in the Superdome before or since." Said lifelong fan Christopher Bravender, "Gleason's play transcends football. Our city was crippled. We needed the Saints and we needed them desperately. We needed the distraction. We needed the inspiration. We needed to feel like we were part of something. That blocked punt literally helped people rebuild their homes. It symbolized being back."

Gleason was an improbable hero. He was small in size, had limited physical gifts, and was never a full-time starter. He wore his hair long, loved local music, and rode around town on a bicycle. Less a sports star, Gleason seemed more like everyone else in New Orleans.

The permanent portrayal of that fateful play has taken on the name the Rebirth Statue. Steve Gleason himself has said that it represents "coming through adversity. It's about finding your heroes. It's about commitment and a rebirth for all."

Address Mercedes-Benz Superdome, 1500 Sugar Bowl Drive, New Orleans, LA 70112, +1 504.587.3822 | Tip Until the Saints finally won a Super Bowl in 2010, they'd been considered a historically bad team. Since the Superdome is built on land that was once the Girod Cemetery from 1822 to 1957, many felt the team was cursed from their inception in 1967 because they played on haunted burial grounds.

86 __ Ricca's Architectural Sales
Salvaging the history of New Orleans

Peter Ricca could be considered the Mr. Wreck-It of New Orleans. His company demolished more than 14 blocks of commercial buildings to make way for the widening of Poydras Street in the 1960s. He also razed the former public library at Lee Circle, plus a few seen-better-days mansions along St. Charles Avenue, the Holy Family Convent on Orleans Street, the Soniat Memorial at the old Mercy Hospital on Annunciation Street, the New Orleans Home for Incurables on Henry Clay Avenue, and maybe most famously, the Higgins Industries plant on City Park Avenue, where the PT boats used at Normandy Beach on D-Day were designed and built.

But he wasn't just a wrecker. Ricca's company is, as their slogan states, "Working to Preserve New Orleans' Architectural Heritage." Since 1956, Ricca's has saved much of what they tore down in a small warehouse in the backstreets of Mid-City. On display and up for sale is a treasure trove of salvaged architectural goods. They have a huge selection of oversized doors, vintage lighting, antique wrought-iron fountains, garden benches, claw-foot tubs, old and ornately designed metal gates and fences, door knockers, glass and crystal doorknobs, the noted iron horse-head posts you'll see around the city, and oval Victorian foundation vents. You can even find refurbished skeleton-key locks. If you've been looking "forever" for hard-to-find and no-longer-produced hinges or bolts, Ricca's probably has them.

If you go to the warehouse on North Solomon Street, a total back alley, you must use caution. Crime is not the concern, but the car-devouring potholes are. Unlike most of America, built on bedrock, New Orleans is built on Mississippi River silt. What you will experience as new potholes and new sidewalk bricks out of place every day is not negligence or lack of public funds. It's simply one of the hardships of living in a city built upon a swamp.

Address 511 N Solomon Street, New Orleans, LA 70119, +1 504.488.5524,
www.riccasarchitecturalsales.com | **Hours** Tue – Sat 9am – 5pm | **Tip** Just around the corner
from Ricca's is Creole Country (512 David St) a meat lover's shrine oddly situated inside
a shotgun house in an otherwise 100 percent residential neighborhood. Fab and Ricker
Schmitt opened their Cajun charcuterie in 1979. Their son, Vaughn, runs it today. Here
you can pick up andouille sausage, alligator meat, tasso, and headcheese, as well as more
"normal" cuts.

87 __ Riverfront Monuments

Honoring old men, nude men, and men we'd like to forget

New Orleans riverfront is not lined with gift shops like Paseo del Rio in San Antonio, or cluttered with bars like the Flats in Cleveland. Being below sea level, the New Orleans river walk has a large gray wall on one side so residents don't drown. On the other side is the Mississippi, nicknamed the Big Muddy for a reason.

There is a brick riverside path that runs the breadth of the French Quarter from Canal Street to Governor Nicholls Street. Along the walkway are many commemorative statues. Among them is a seated bronze man in a suit with a young boy, who looks very much like the old man's mini-me. The sculpture actually depicts Malcolm Woldenberg – a philanthropist who helped fund the surrounding park – and his grandnephew, and was created by artist William Ludwig in 1990. The *Monument to the Immigrants* was unveiled in 1995. Franco Allesandrini's white marble statue depicts Miss Liberty facing the river while one of the many immigrant families who made New Orleans faces the French Quarter. An 18-foot sculpture of a powerfully built nude man with no hands or legs below the knees, called *Old Man River*, bears a plaque that reads: "A Man with a Past / Arms reach empty handed, / God to a city in Love / with Water."

There is one monument that keeps moving and being altered, almost as if the city is embarrassed by it. It is. *The Battle of Liberty Place* was erected to honor the Crescent City White League, a racist group of ex-Confederates who overthrew the state government in 1874. The monument was prominently placed at the foot of Canal Street in 1891. Inscriptions honoring white supremacy were added in 1932 and later removed in the 1980s. The entire monument was dug up and removed in 1989 when the city council declared it a nuisance and relegated it to a warehouse. Yet somehow, the Liberty Place monument snuck back and is now on display, tucked behind the Audubon Aquarium.

MONUMENT
TO THE
IMMIGRANT

DEDICATED
TO THE
COURAGEOUS MEN AND WOMEN
WHO LEFT THEIR HOMELAND
SEEKING FREEDOM, OPPORTUNITY
AND A BETTER LIFE IN A NEW COUNTRY.

MARCH 19, 1995

Address Statues are located along the riverfront path from Canal to Toulouse Streets | **Tip** The steamboat *Natchez*, docked at the base of Toulouse St, is in its ninth generation. The original *Natchez* was built in 1823. The sixth one beat the *Robert E. Lee* in history's most famous steamboat race. Today's *Natchez* is one of only two true steam-powered boats in the United States. Two-hour tours are available three times per day.

88 Roman Candy Cart
Strolling sweets

First-time visitors come to New Orleans seemingly very familiar with pralines, beignets, and Lucky Dog carts. Lesser known but equally important to the city's street-food story is the Roman Candy Cart.

Roman Candy is a taffy stick originally made by Angelina Napoli Cortese in her home kitchen in the early 20th century and served to family and friends on special occasions like Christmas and St. Joseph's Day. It was called "Roman" due to some anti-Italian sentiment at the time.

After losing both legs below the knees in a streetcar accident, Angelina's 12-year-old son, Sam, sold fruit and vegetables from a goat-drawn cart. He would often bring leftovers of his mother's taffy to sell on his wagon. The candy always sold well and customers began to request it, so Sam decided to start peddling the confections on a regular basis. He drew up a design for a special mule-drawn candy cart with a wheelwright named Tom Brinker. The two launched the new company in 1915, selling vanilla, chocolate, and strawberry taffy for five cents a stick. For 55 years, the price stayed the same. Today, a stick will set you back $1, but the original three flavors are still all that are sold off the back of that same carriage with the distinctive red-spoked wheels.

After Sam's death in 1969, his grandson Ron Kottemann took over the business, and he continues to this day. Kottemann began making rounds with his grandfather as a young boy. In those years, the cart traveled throughout the city, ferrying across the Industrial Canal to reach Chalmette and the Mississippi to sell in Algiers.

You can now track the Roman Candy cart's day-to-day location via Facebook. It is most common to find the mule half asleep and the cart parked in a shady spot along St. Charles Avenue in Uptown. In the mid-1980s, Kotteman added a second cart at a permanent location inside the Audubon Zoo, just outside the primates' exhibit.

Address Sells from various spots throughout New Orleans, www.romancandy.com, Facebook: Roman Candy | **Hours** Check Facebook for location and hours | **Tip** For considerably more than $1, you can ride a mule-drawn carriage through the French Quarter. Once the only mode of transport through the city, they are lined up and waiting on Decatur St in front of Jackson Square. Be warned: local motorists will curse you as the slow-moving carriages clog the narrow streets.

89 __ The Roosevelt Hotel

A luxury hotel with a legendary history

Entering through the revolving doors, the Roosevelt Hotel looks and even smells like old money, a place where wealthy New Orleans families might once have met Granddaddy and Nana for Sunday brunch.

The hotel, which opened in 1893, was originally called the Grunewald, after its German builder, but was renamed the Roosevelt in 1923, in honor of the U.S. President. Then, in 1965, it was bought by a hotel group and rechristened the Fairmont. Locals paid no attention and continued to call it the Roosevelt. After the 2005 flood, the hotel remained vacant for more than two years, an abandoned eyesore in the post-Katrina landscape. Eventually, Sam Friedman, son of a Louisiana senator, orchestrated a buyout by the Waldorf Astoria. The Waldorf spent more than $170 million to restore the Roosevelt, giving a piece of history back to New Orleans.

The hotel's storied past includes the Cave, the first nightclub in America where chorus girls danced to Dixieland Jazz under fabricated stalactites and waterfalls. The Cave is no longer, but the Blue Room remains. It was a supper club and host to performers like Frank Sinatra, Ray Charles, Ella Fitzgerald, Jimmy Durante, and Louis Armstrong. The hotel also houses the Sazerac Bar, where the locally famous sazerac cocktail may or may not have been invented.

The entire 12th floor used to be occupied by Louisiana's beautifully corrupt governor, Huey P. Long. He used the Roosevelt for various nefarious political activities and personal pleasures. He was assassinated in 1937, but his locked donation box still graces the lobby. Slipping bills in Huey's box today may not bring you luck and probably won't buy influence, but it's still a better bet than the nearby Harrah's Casino.

If you're in New Orleans at Christmastime, the exquisitely decked-out lobby is a must-visit, and the hotel also hosts the Teddy Bear Tea for children, which garners raves but might run you more than your last two paychecks.

Address 130 Roosevelt Way, New Orleans, LA 70112, +1 504.648.1200, www.therooseveltneworleans.com | **Tip** Other holiday traditions in New Orleans include: réveillon dinners, a French Creole custom in which restaurants offer prix fixe menus that include absinthe oyster soup and sugarcane smoked Muscovy duck breast; *feux de joie*, a Cajun ritual of setting massive bonfires along the banks of the Mississippi to light the way for Papa Nöel, the Cajun Santa Claus; the free Christmas Concert Series at the St. Louis Cathedral; and caroling at Jackson Square by candlelight.

90__Rosalie Alley

Walk softly and carry a big Zulian stick

Sounding like a test of faith, Rosalie Alley lies midway between Piety and Desire (Streets). It's a slim grass-covered corridor between houses in the middle of the 3300 block of North Rampart Street in the Bywater. You'd barely notice it if not for the ever-evolving fence paintings of grinning skeletons (often wearing top hats, sometimes smoking cigars), painted roses, hearts, ornate Christian crosses, the ubiquitous three X's, and odd enigmatic phrases in Spanish like *Recemos Nos Para Nuestros Art Pasados*, which literally translates as "We pray for our art past."

On many Saturday evenings, Rosalie Alley comes alive with people, mostly dressed in white and red, walking the path while chanting and swaying to the sounds of the conga drum. These are members of La Source Anciene, New Orleans' most active Voodoo congregation, led by mambo Sally Ann Glassman, who studied Voodoo in Haiti. While the Roman Catholic archdiocese of New Orleans does not recognize Voodoo as a legitimate religion (even the plaque on the tomb of NOLA's most famous Voodoo priestess, Marie Laveau, states she practiced the "cult" of Voodoo), the Catholic Church in the Vatican officially recognized Voodoo as an ancestor-worship-based faith back in 1960. Pope John Paul II even attended Voodoo ceremonies in Togo, Africa, in 1985 and Benin in 1993.

If you show up for a Saturday ritual with a large group, you'll likely receive a less-than-gracious reception; one or two people, however, should be fine. The ceremonies are peaceful and benevolent. You'll neither witness nor be dragged into any bizarre rites involving hexes or animal sacrifice. You might think about bringing some small gifts to honor the space and to please the spirits. Typical offerings are flowers, plants, candles, or religious statues or pictures. If you decoupaged the image of a Loa or the Black Madonna, that might be considered a bit much for a first timer.

Address 3319 Rosalie Alley, New Orleans, LA 70117 | **Tip** Rosalie Alley is mere blocks from New Orleans' number-one pizza parlor. Pizza Delicious (617 Piety St) was established by Greg Augarten and Mike Friedman, two guys from New York City who came to college at Tulane and fell in love with the city but thought the pizza sucked. So, they decided to stick around and open a pizza place themselves.

91_Royal Street Musicians
Street crescendo

Each day the section of Royal Street between St. Ann and St. Louis Streets is closed off from car traffic from 11am to 4pm, making it essentially a pedestrian mall. During these hours, the three-block stretch is lined with magicians, mimes, and performers of all kinds. The top draws, however, are the street musicians.

A number of NOLA's most noted musicians got their starts on Royal Street. A young Henry Byrd found a discarded piano in the alley and began banging out tunes on the French Quarter pavement. He would go on to become Professor Longhair, the originator of the "New Orleans Sound," a vivacious form of a rhumba-rhythmed piano blues. Meschiya Lake, named best female vocalist in the city from 2012 to 2014, sang for tips on Royal before hitting the big time – cutting three award-winning CDs and touring internationally. Louis Michot, a member of the Lost Bayou Ramblers, said, "It was a huge part of my musical training. I learned how to connect my music with the people hearing it on the street. That's just so New Orleans."

Because of the transient nature of buskers, it's hard to pin down who will be playing where and when, but, as they say, it's all good. If you're lucky, you might catch Tanya & Dorise, a popular duet who often perform on weekends near St. Louis Street. The violin-playing Tanya is thought to be the inspiration for the character Annie in HBO's *Tremé*. Another family act features acclaimed clarinetist Doreen Ketchens; her husband, Lawrence, on tuba, trombone, and piano; and their daughter Dorian on drums. They play traditional New Orleans-style jazz in front of Rouses market near St. Peter Street.

But the unrivaled star of Royal Street is Grandpa Elliott. Looking like Uncle Remus with his white beard, red shirt, straw hat, and overalls, the nearly blind singer and harmonica player can be found most days at the corner of Toulouse and Royal.

Address Royal Street between St. Ann and St. Louis Streets, New Orleans, LA 70116 | **Tip** When handing out quarters and dollars on the street, don't give anything to the guy painted silver with a handlebar mustache seated near Jackson Square. He is rumored to have collected more than $30,000 in one year because people felt he was great at being a statue. He *is* a statue. Some guy just painted a mannequin silver and sits nearby to watch his tip bucket.

92 Sacred Grinds

Graves and green tea

New Orleans may no longer have a streetcar named Desire (the inspiration for Tennessee Williams' iconic play), but since the reopening of the Canal Street line, in 2004, the city does have a streetcar named Cemeteries. The "Cemeteries" streetcar leaves from the foot of Canal Street downtown and runs to City Park Avenue, where there are more than a half dozen cemeteries within walking distance. If the roughly 20-minute ride past residential and commercial areas gets your taste buds or thirst going, hop off at Sacred Grinds, an unusual coffee shop located at the end of the route.

Nestled between St. Patrick Cemetery No. 2 and Odd Fellows Rest, and housed inside the Herb Import Company, the tiny cafe with the motto "Coffee to Wake the Dead" provides a nice respite before or after your cemetery visits. It's a tight squeeze for humans (and their four-legged friends, as Sacred Grinds is dog friendly) with eight small tables in the back, facing St. Patrick No. 2, and eight tables facing Canal Street and the Katrina Memorial. With tombs as your backdrop no matter where you sit, it's the perfect place to enjoy the beverage of your choice and an artichoke brioche while pondering your mortality (but not the wonders of air-conditioning, as all seating is outside). Their specialty drink is the Dirty Zombie–a frozen chocolate malt with espresso–and their pastries arrive daily from local bakeries around the city.

If you're hoping to extend your mortality, the Herb Import Company offers organic teas, essential oils, herbal vaporizers, aromatherapy, detox powders, Day of the Dead paraphilia, and even Voodoo flags to chase evil spirits away. There is also a nice selection of alternative magazines and books that you can read to pass the time while nearby, people get on and off the streetcar at the spot where, for the living (as for the dead), "Cemeteries" is the last stop.

Address 5055 Canal Street, New Orleans, LA 70119, +1 504.488.4889, www.sacredgrinds.com | **Hours** Mon–Sat 7am–7pm, Sun 7am–6pm | **Tip** Directly across the street is the Katrina Memorial, in Charity Hospital Cemetery (5056 Canal St). Dedicated in 2008, it is the final resting place for 85 hurricane victims who were never identified. A monument symbolizing the eye of the storm is the centerpiece, with curving walkways around it to signify the high-velocity winds.

93 _ Sam the Banana Man's House

Home of presidents and presidential overthrows

Visitors ride the St. Charles streetcar in droves to see the large historic homes that line the avenue. Among the most impressive is a grand mansion right next to Tulane that seems to have bought Ionic columns on sale, buy 10 get 2 free. It currently houses the president of the university, but was once the home of Sam "the Banana Man" Zemurray, one of Tulane's greatest benefactors and the poster child for both the merits and perils of American capitalism.

Sam was a Russian-Jewish immigrant, uneducated, near penniless, but in possession of a hunger to make it in his new country. At 17, Sam observed dockworkers for the Boston Fruit Company discarding the no longer green bananas and used his last $140 to buy up all the ripe rejects. He loaded them into a rented boxcar and telegraphed the grocers to alert them he'd be passing through their towns with ripe bananas at discount prices. From these humble beginnings, Sam went on to run the United Fruit Company, with the largest private fleet of ships in the world, 83,000 employees, and over 250,000 acres for the cultivation of bananas, sugar cane, and cacao.

In order to keep his business growing in size and profits, Sam was not afraid to fight dirty. In 1953, he famously instigated the removal of the president of Guatemala, Jacobo Árbenz, when Árbenz attempted to expropriate land owned by United Fruit and redistribute it to local peasants. Sam hired an ad agency to spread propaganda about Árbenz in order to convince the U.S. government that Guatemala was becoming a puppet for the Soviets. It worked. The CIA ended up staging a coup that replaced Árbenz, and United Fruit's land was secured.

The many tales – both sordid and fascinating – about the life of Sam Zemurray could fill a book. In fact they did; Sam's story is brilliantly retold in Rich Cohen's biography *The Fish That Ate the Whale*.

Address 7000 St. Charles Street, New Orleans, LA 70118 | Hours Not open to the public; viewable from the outside only | Tip Another jewel along St. Charles is the Columns Hotel (3811 St. Charles Ave). It was built in 1883 for the owner of Hernsheim Brothers & Co., the largest manufacturer of cigars in the States. One of the great pleasures is to sit out on the large front veranda with a whiskey and a cigar and watch the streetcars roll by.

94_ The School of Burlesque

Pay attention to draw attention

The New Orleans School of Burlesque was started in 2008 in a small studio across the Mississippi River on the Westbank, or what locals call the Wank. What was conceived as possibly a one-time-only event has blossomed into the city's only school specializing in the modern art of burlesque.

There are one-hour walk-in classes every week that are open to all. Just shove your insecurities in a small (or massive) box and go on in. Yes, men are welcome too. Classes start at a mere $10, and you can learn everything from dance steps to costume creation to character development. The school offers ongoing workshops and frequently has renowned performers from the city and beyond as guest teachers. The private group sessions have become popular as energetic alternatives to traditional bachelorette or birthday parties. (Note to conference or convention attendees: this would be a hell of a lot more fun than any of those boring "team building" activities being planned by your HR director.)

The school was founded and is led by headmistress Bella Blue. Bella is a native New Orleanian who's been dancing since the age of three (obviously more naïve than naughty in the early years). Today she's considered one of the international stars of burlesque, and was even named one of the world's top 50 burlesque artists by *21st Century* magazine. Which is all to say: learning burlesque from Bella in New Orleans is akin to being taught how to throw a football by Drew Brees.

Locally, Bella is the artistic director of numerous burlesque shows around town, including "The Dirty Dime Peepshow," "Strip Roulette," and "The Blue Book Cabaret." The last was the subject of a much publicized story when Lucky Pierre's fired one of the performers for being too voluptuous. Bella moved her show to another venue in what was seen as a virtuous "girl power" moment.

Address 2732 St. Claude Ave. Ste 256 (inside the New Orleans Healing Center), New Orleans, LA 70116, +1 504.912.1734, www.nolaschoolofburlesque.com | Hours Check website for class schedule; private sessions by appointment | Tip Now that you've silenced your inhibitions, you might want to hit the karaoke bars. Kajun's Pub (2256 St. Claude Ave) has more than 50,000 catalogued songs, including some by Pee-Wee Herman. It is considered New Orleans' top spot to get your karaoke on.

95 __ Southern Food and Beverage Museum

Where to explore cuisine of consequence

The Southern Food and Beverage Museum is a nonprofit dedicated to the understanding and celebration of Southern cuisine. While there exist museums devoted to specific food products – SPAM (in Minnesota), Dr Pepper (in Texas), and mustard (in Wisconsin) – the SoFAB Institute is the only generalized food museum in America.

Founded in 2008, the museum survived its first years housed in the wretched Riverwalk Mall. When the mall was closed and replaced by the Riverwalk Marketplace, SoFAB moved into the former Dryades Street Market in Central City. The museum occupies roughly 12,000 square feet, with about 1800 square feet set aside for temporary exhibits.

The Leah Chase Louisiana Gallery features a permanent exhibit focused on the food and traditions of Louisiana. Named after one of New Orleans' premier Creole chefs, the gallery showcases everything from beignets and crawfish to the evolution of jambalaya from colonial times. The Gallery of the South presents mini exhibits that explore the flavors and cuisines of each Southern state. Individual state signs have been designed and created by New Orleans' favorite folk artist, Dr. Bob (see p. 58).

Events at SoFAB range from weekly cooking demonstrations to spirit tastings and lively lectures on subjects like the origins of Creole cuisine. SoFAB also incorporates the Museum of the American Cocktail, which celebrates mixology from its origins to the present day, and houses a reference library containing an extensive collection of Southern cookbooks and the menus of iconic restaurants, as well as culinary books of all kinds. After you're done reading, learning, and hearing about Southern food, you can walk past a curtained wall to actually eat in the museum's on-site restaurant, Purloo.

Address 1504 Oretha Castle Haley Boulevard, New Orleans, LA 70113, +1 504.569.0405, www.sofabinstitute.org | Hours Thu–Mon 11am–5:30pm | Tip In addition to visiting the food museum you can buy 17th- through 19th-century artifacts at Lucullus (610 Chartres St), an unusual shop specializing in culinary antiques. Check out the silver settings, centuries-old dining tables, hand-blown glasses and fine crystal champagne flutes, and, of course, absinthe paraphernalia.

96_ Spanish Stables
The truth is out there ... on a plaque

The poorly named Old Spanish Stables were only very briefly used as stables and were never Spanish at all. Designed by Henry Latrobe, the building has transferred ownership 15 times since 1804. When Francis Gallier Preval bought it, he finally converted the first floor into a small stable in 1835, more than 30 years after Spanish rule left New Orleans.

In 1962, Clay Shaw purchased the historic property. Shaw was a highly decorated war hero, who was known locally for following his passion to restore French Quarter architecture, including the French Market. Despite his good standing in the community, Shaw became the unwitting victim of the city's then district attorney, Jim Garrison, who, were there ever such a competition, would be a top contender for the worst person in New Orleans' history.

Garrison wanted to challenge the Warren Commission's report on JFK's assassination, largely because he saw an opportunity to make himself a national name. He was intrigued by Lee Harvey Oswald's connections to New Orleans and cynically chose Shaw as his prosecutorial target. To tie Shaw to the crime, Garrison's office bullied witnesses into providing false testimony. Behind the scenes, Garrison slipped concocted lies to journalists, for instance that he thought the crime was a "homosexual thrill killing."

After dragging Shaw through the mud, Garrison's case ended in an acquittal after less than one hour of deliberation, or "long enough for them to take a bathroom break," as the daughter of one of Shaw's attorneys put it years later. The plaque affixed to the non-Spanish non-Stables remains the one true testimony to Clay Shaw. It reads, "Pioneer in the renovation of the Vieux Carré ... Clay Shaw was a patron of the humanities and lived his life with the utmost grace; an invaluable citizen, he was respected, admired, and loved by many."

Address 724 Governor Nicholls Street, New Orleans, LA 70116 | Hours Not open to the public; viewable from the outside only | Tip Before Garrison's made-up case, New Orleans' biggest liar was John Law. The convicted murderer and gambler sought immigrant workers to increase the value of his Louisiana land holdings and lured them to New Orleans with exaggerated claims of an idyllic setting rather than the humid, snake-infested swamp it was.

97__St. Expedite

When you need a miracle – STAT

Far less visited than St. Louis Cemetery No. 1 is the Our Lady of Guadalupe Church (also known as the Mortuary Chapel), located across the street. The church was built in 1826 out of necessity to hold the bodies of the many yellow fever victims. Back then, the corpses were (incorrectly) thought to be highly contagious and were therefore stored and separated away from the living.

Although the famous St. Louis Cathedral (1720), a few blocks away on Jackson Square, has burned down and been rebuilt once and altered several times, the Mortuary Chapel is actually the oldest intact church in the city. The church has semi-frequent but always fabulous jazz masses. And to the side of the chapel is a small grotto lined with plaster thank-you plaques. But the number-one reason to visit is the statue of St. Expedite inside the church.

Churches used to order their statues of Jesus, Mary, and the saints from Italy or Spain. The statues would arrive in crates marked with the name of the enclosed holy figure. One crate received by Our Lady of Guadalupe had the word "Expedite" written on the outside. The intended message was "Open Immediately," but the recipients incorrectly interpreted the label as being the name of the saint packed inside. And so the statue of "St. Expedite," in his Roman soldier garb, stands at the back of the church, on the far right as you enter.

St. Expedite is recognized as the patron saint of quick results. For reasons that are not clear, you're supposed to leave him pound cake after he's interceded on your behalf. While not officially sanctioned by the Catholic Church, St. Expedite's fame and influence are enjoying a recent surge as computer software and tech workers have been invoking him for faster connections. In the gift shop, attached to the church, you may purchase St. Expedite prayer cards or medals. The medals can be attached to your keychain for fast getaways.

Address 411 N Rampart Street, New Orleans, LA 70112, +1 504.525.1551, www.judesshrine.com | **Hours** Mass: Sun 7:30am, 9:30am, 11:30am, 1:30pm (Spanish), and 6pm; weekdays 7am, noon; Sat 7am; Sat Vigil 4pm | **Tip** A few blocks away is the setting for an event far less holy. Back in 2006, Zach Bowen took his life by jumping off the roof of a hotel. In his pocket was a note indicating where to find his girlfriend, Addie Hall. She was back in their apartment at 828 N Rampart St, above the Voodoo Temple. Her torso was found in the fridge. Her head, hands, and feet were in pots on the stove. And her legs were in the oven – they had been seasoned.

"ST. EXPEDITE"
PRAY FOR US

98_ St. Roch Grotto

A chapel with heart … and feet, and brains

There are 38 cemeteries in New Orleans. Most visitors will venture into St. Louis No.1, where Marie Laveau is buried in the second most visited gravesite in America (Elvis' tomb in Memphis is the first). Actor Nicolas Cage will one day be interred in St. Louis No.1. His chosen vault is easy to identify because of the lipstick kisses blanketed across the front. Film studios seem to prefer Lafayette No.1 in the Garden District, which has been used as a ready-made set in many movies, including *Interview with a Vampire*.

But one of the coolest, if lesser known, spots is the grotto inside the chapel found in the St. Roch Cemetery. The small room is filled with tokens of gratitude for illnesses that have been cured: plaques etched with "Thanks" or "Merci," ancient abandoned leg braces and crutches that look more like torture devices, plaster and cement statues of previously afflicted body parts – hands, feet, hearts, brains – all healed through prayer at St. Roch's. There are often left-behind silk flowers, handwritten notes, and photographs of loved ones.

In 1867, Father Peter Leonard Thevis arrived from Germany to minister to the neighborhood's predominantly German parishioners. The area was once called "Little Saxony." Yellow fever had killed more than 3000 in New Orleans that year. Father Pete gathered his congregation and together they prayed to St. Roch, the patron saint of dogs, plague, and pestilence, to intercede on their behalf. When not one parishioner subsequently contracted the disease, he began raising money to build a shrine to the saint. It was completed in August 1876.

The cemetery outside the grotto is lined with 14 tableaus representing the stations of the cross. Life-sized and brilliantly white statues are set against teal-painted backgrounds. Bring your camera and, if you're suffering from a hangover, may I suggest a plaster cast of a brain?

Address 1725 St. Roch Avenue, New Orleans, LA 70117 | **Hours** Mon–Fri 8:30am–4pm, closed Sat and Sun | **Tip** The Sunday mass at the adjoining church, Our Lady Star of the Sea Catholic Church, is quite an experience. Priest Tony Ricard is a huge NFL Saints fan. During one mass, he ripped off his clerical robes to reveal a Saints jersey, and the choir broke into "The Crunk Song" – the football team's anthem. The congregation popped open their black-and-gold umbrellas, and the whole church did a second-line parade down the aisle.

99 ___ St. Roch Market

A food court for foodies

St. Roch Market officially reopened April 10, 2015, after being shuttered for 10 years following Hurricane Katrina. When the original market opened in 1875, in the pre-grocery store era, St. Roch's was a place to grab a pound of shrimp and a dozen eggs laid by yard chickens. Joining the throngs on the new market's inaugural weekend, a 50-something woman remembered: "My mother and I came here every Saturday to get gladiolas for my grandparents' graves – it had to be gladiolas – and produce for the week."

St. Roch's is not your typical urban market. The concept is upscale – some might say haute cuisine – but at affordable prices. The revitalized emporium is a bright, white and airy space featuring the building's original columns. There are high tables and stools in the center at which to dine, converse, or take it all in.

There are 13 food vendors lining the sides of the market, ranging from a specialty butcher to a raw oyster bar. Among the prepared-food vendors is Micah Martello, a New Orleans native, returned after several years running the King Creole food truck. His menu features items like shrimp and grits and crawfish poutine, a Cajun spin on a Canadian recipe, mixing crawfish with french fries, cheese curd, and a roast-beef gravy. The next stall, Koreole, purveys an inventive fusion of Korean and Creole cuisines. Try the "Japchalaya" (andouille sausage, vermicelli noodles, and vegetables).

Inside the front door, St. Roch Forage sells vegetables and flowers from local urban growers. You can purchase fresh groceries or sign up for a weekly produce box. In the adjoining stall, Juice NOLA uses the fruits and veggies from Forage to create unique salads and cold-pressed juices right in front of you.

Even without buying a thing, St. Roch Market is a great place to drink in the bustle of an urban marketplace – plus there's seating front and back, out in the open air.

Address 2381 St. Claude Avenue, New Orleans, LA 70117, +1(504) 609-3813, www.strochmarket.com | Hours Daily 7am–11pm | Tip If you desire a more typical grocery store experience, the Rouses chain is the Louisiana-based version of Kroger or Piggly Wiggly. And Langenstein's (1330 Arabella St), around since 1922, sells a variety of prepared foods and brands not seen anywhere else.

100__ Steamboat Houses

One man's home is his cruise ship

Visitors to New Orleans tend to focus on the architecture in two areas of the city, the French Quarter and the Garden District. Yet out in the neighborhood of Holy Cross in the Lower Ninth Ward, the pair of steamboat houses may be the most uniquely designed homes in the entire city. Very few venture there, however. In fact, current owner of one of the houses, Emile Dumesnil, has said more boats on the river pass by his address than cars on the street.

The first steamboat house was built in 1905 for Milton Doullut and his wife. Both were riverboat captains. Seven years later, the Doullots had a similar house built for their son Paul across the street. The two houses were designated historic landmarks in 1977.

Both three-story houses could be called Steamboat Gothic, with their wraparound porches accented by huge carved cypress balls, which resemble either a pearl necklace or a string of white Mardi Gras beads, depending on your orientation. From a distance, they also look like decorative bunting on a ship about to leave port. Oval stained-glass windows, like portholes, are posted at each corner. The pagoda-style roofs may have been influenced by the Japanese exhibit at the 1904 World's Fair in St. Louis. They are trimmed with ornate ironwork and have two metal smokestacks instead of chimneys. These were both knocked down, one during Hurricane Katrina, the other during Rita, and have since been restored.

The interiors have as many architectural quirks as the exteriors. Pocket doors divide all interior rooms. The walls and ceilings are covered in embossed-metal panels. But the most interesting – i.e., weird – details are on the ground floor, where all the walls and floors are completely tiled. This came in particularly handy when Hurricane Katrina left five feet of standing water in the homes. Because there was no exposed wood or plaster, once the water receded, the first floor could basically be hosed out and reoccupied right away.

Address 400 and 503 Egania Street (Lower Ninth Ward), New Orleans, LA 70117 |
Hours Not open to the public; viewable from the outside only | Tip On the front of many
homes in the Ninth Ward there remains the Katrina stamp. FEMA and rescue workers
went house to house after the flood, looking for survivors or dealing with the dead. After
inspection, each house received a spray painted X with each quadrant carrying specific
information. The top displays the date the house was searched. The left side identifies the
rescue team, the right indicates any hazards present, and the lower quadrant is the most
somber notation, the number of dead bodies found on site.

101_ Street Tiles

History at your feet

New Orleanians are passionate about their street names. Less than half of 1 percent of the city's streets are numbered; the vast majority are named after royals, politicians, plantation owners, philanthropists, pirates, and others. The French Quarter is laid out in a grid with its earliest streets named for the bastard children of Louis XIV (Toulouse, Conti, Dumaine, Chartres), interspersed with streets named after various saints.

Many of the streets' pronunciations are often used as signifiers to determine if someone is a local. One of the best ways to be NOLA-ier than thou? Pronounce the following streets the "right" way: Burgundy (bur-*gun*-dee), Milan (*My*-lan), Calliope (*cal*-lee-ope), Euterpe (you-terp), Carondelet (kuh-ran-duh-let), and the mother of all street names, the four-syllable Tchoupitoulas (*chop*-ah-too-luhs). Once you have mastered the pronunciations, it's time to ask for directions.

Don't be surprised if you ask a local what street you are on and they point to the ground. It was not until the early 20th century that the city installed traditional street signs. Before that, people were completely reliant on blue and white tiles manufactured in Belgium and Ohio with street names and addresses on them, embedded in streets and sidewalks.

Some of the original street names remain in the sidewalks. For example, on Oretha Castle Haley Boulevard you can still see "Dryades" underfoot, and places on Tremé Street still show "North Liberty Street." In Mid-City, while the street sign that reads "Hennessey" (for murdered police chief David C. Hennessy) is spelled incorrectly, the street tiles are correct. Following Hurricane Katrina, the city allowed citizens to make their own official street signs and interest in street tiles surged; they became a revered symbol of civic pride. So as you walk around New Orleans, don't just look up and around for art and history – look at your feet.

102 __ Studio Inferno

High art across the tracks

Located just yards across the parish line (and less than eight miles from the French Quarter) is the glass studio and art gallery, Studio Inferno. After more than 20 years in the Bywater, owner and internationally known glass artist Mitchell Gaudet moved Inferno into an old 1947 movie theater in Arabi. The space totals over 12,000 square feet, with a 2500-square-foot gallery and 8000-square-foot glass studio and metal shop.

The gallery hosts rotating exhibitions on a bimonthly basis that feature painters, metalworkers, sculptors, and other artists from around the country, and quite often, around the world. For those interested in glass production, just stop in during working hours and watch Gaudet and his team create some of Inferno's production-line items, which include iconic New Orleans imagery: brightly colored fleur-de-lis, water meters, hoodoo dolls, and sand-cast Mardi Gras maskers infused with symbolism from nature and bacchanalia. There are also hanging monkeys (inspired by the 1960s game Barrel of Monkeys), wineglasses with male and female torsos as stems, and glass pendant necklaces featuring chili peppers, lucky cats, oysters, red beans, and alligators, to name a few.

Using glass for its transparency, beauty, and fragility, Gaudet's own intricate artwork represents his take on history, music, religion, manmade disasters, nature, and the complexity of personal relationships. His collection of various found items is located all over the rear of the studio.

Inferno also does custom jobs (see the cast-glass blue note atop the Musicians Tomb in St. Louis Cemetery No. 1) and commissions of all kinds, from awards to convention gifts to large-scale architectural glass walls (like the one in the Renaissance New Orleans Arts Hotel). The studio is also available for private tours and school groups by appointment.

Address 6601 St. Claude Avenue, New Orleans, LA 70117, +1 504.945.1878, www.facebook.com/infernonola | **Hours** Mon–Sat 10am–4pm. Art openings on select Saturdays 6pm–10pm. The glass furnaces are typically up and running October–May. | **Tip** The Old Arabi Bar (6701 N Peters St), featuring live music, is a neighborhood watering hole where you might find music legends in the audience being goaded onstage for jam sessions. Tuesdays are open-mic nights. And if the music is too loud, buy a tamale, get a go-cup, and stroll on the levee.

103__ The Tattoo Museum

A permanent display for permanent ink

Tattoo artist "Doc" Don Lucas is a legendary figure in the field. He spent his long career in the trade traveling the world, gathering both stories and artifacts. He was born and raised near a naval shipyard in California and started his tattoo apprenticeship in 1972 under "Rangoon" Ricky Bordeaux. In 1983, Lucas moved to New Orleans and opened a studio when tattoos were far more fringe than they are today. He recalls that back then, "the city disliked you, the police hated you, nobody wanted you to move next door – you were a pariah."

Among Lucas' protégés was Henri Montegut, whose son, Adam, followed in his career path. Adam came to share Lucas' passion for preserving the history and traditions of tattoos, and used Kickstarter and other funding sources to create a 2000-square-foot ode to ink in the form of a tattoo museum and studio. The space is divided into three sections. The gallery displays contemporary tattoo art and the work of non-tattoo artists, like Ralph Steadman, deeply admired by the owners. The tattoo parlor offers the services of Adam and other gifted artists. The museum features rotating exhibits, showcasing items from the collection of Doc Don. These include 60 years' worth of designs by famed skin artist George Webb. Webb's "flash" paintings – punctured hearts, skulls, daggers wrapped in banners – line the museum's entrance.

Inside display cases you'll find a variety of paraphernalia and vintage objects, from old tattoo guns and pigment bottles to framed photographs of inked carnival sideshow performers and the original paintings and drawings of legendary tattoo artists. There's also a collection of taxidermy animals, which seem to have nothing to do with the museum but are cool nonetheless.

The stunning logo for the museum, designed by Adam, is available on T-shirts, posters (some signed), and burned into wood with a wax seal of authenticity.

Address 1915-1/2 Martin Luther King Jr. Boulevard, New Orleans, LA 70113, +1 504.218.5319, www.nolatattoomuseum.com | Hours Tue–Sat 1pm–7pm, Mon by appointment, closed Sun | Tip There are more than 75 tattoo parlors in the metro area. Electric Ladyland (610 Frenchmen St) employs the most artists and is the most popular. Aart Accent (1041 N Rampart St) is the most venerable. Owner Jacci Gresham, the first female black tattoo artist in the United States, opened her shop in 1976.

104_ Tomb of the Unknown Slave

A touchingly undistinguished monument

In the 1830s, free people of color in New Orleans sought and received permission from Bishop Antoine Blanc to build a church. Ursuline's agreed to donate the property at what is now Governor Nicholls Street and St. Claude Avenue, provided the church be named after their founder, St. Angela Merici. The church was finally completed in 1842 and dedicated to St. Augustine. Maybe they forgot the deal.

St. Augustine is the oldest African American Catholic church in the country. Except for a short period in 1925, when its sanctuary was being enlarged, the church has been in continuous use since its founding.

In 1992, William Savoy, rector of St. Luke Episcopal Church in New York, wrote to Father Jerome LeDoux of St. Augustine suggesting that a memorial be erected on church grounds in honor of the countless slaves buried in unmarked graves in New Orleans and all over the country.

Ideas for the memorial went through many visions and revisions. Anna Ross Twichell, a historic preservationist, felt that the elaborate shrines being proposed seemed inappropriate to honor people who had nothing. A plain cross, made from chains and shackles, was chosen to best depict the reality and tragedy of slavery. A heavy rusted marine chain was salvaged locally and cut into two pieces to form the cross. Each link weighs 45 pounds.

The massive unadorned cross is located alongside the church. The plaque at the Tomb of the Unknown Slave reads: *On this October 30, 2004, we, the Faith Community of St. Augustine Catholic Church, dedicate this shrine consisting of grave crosses, chains and shackles to the memory of the nameless, faceless, turfless Africans who met an untimely death in Faubourg Treme .... The Tomb of the Unknown Slave is a constant reminder that we are walking on holy ground.*

Address 1210 Governor Nicholls Street, New Orleans, LA 70116, +1 504.525.5934 | **Tip** St. Augustine Church has only one mass on Sunday, at 10am. It is one of the more interesting as it's often accompanied by gospel music and attended by people of all faiths.

105 _ The Umbrella Girl
Existential graffiti

In 2008, Hurricane Gustav swept through New Orleans as residents and tourists swept out, and one particular visitor swept in: famed British street artist Banksy. The elusive artist alighted in the city, creating over a dozen stenciled paintings on and around the cityscape: a child flying a refrigerator-shaped kite; a young boy swinging on a tire swing (life preserver); a homeless Abraham Lincoln pushing a shopping cart. Some of the images were quickly painted over or literally torn or cut from the exteriors of dilapidated houses.

To date, only three of Banksy's pieces remain in the city. The most popular, which residents call the "Umbrella Girl," is located on the exterior of the old Drop-In Center, an organization that provided medical and social services for runaway and homeless youths. The stencil features a mournful-looking young girl trying to shelter herself from the rain by holding a giant umbrella. The joke is on her, however, because the umbrella is the source of the rain. Many residents see Umbrella Girl's existential situation as a poignant representation of New Orleanians' views on levee protection.

In 2014, thieves posing as art handlers from Los Angeles tried to remove the painting from the cinder-block building with jackhammers and drills in broad daylight. They put up a wooden wall to shield their activity, but curious passersby peeked behind and started asking questions. The men claimed it was going to the Tate Modern Museum in London. Residents posted photos of the theft on social media, the building owners were contacted, and the men fled. A guard was stationed to watch over the painting, and it was plastered back into the wall.

This was not the first incident the resilient Umbrella Girl survived, as she had already suffered other attempts to deface her. Today she still stands, waiting in vain for the rain to stop, on display for anyone who wishes to see her … at least for now.

Address 8131 Hampson Street, New Orleans, LA 70118 | **Tip** Banksy's other two surviving paintings in New Orleans can be found on the corner of Clio and Carondelet Sts and on Jackson Ave between St. Thomas and Rousseau Sts.

106__Ursuline Convent
Storied ground for the sacred and profane

The Ursuline Convent has a long and twisted history. The story begins in 1726, when King Louis XV sent nuns from Rouen to the colony to establish a hospital for the poor and a school for young girls. Fourteen sisters made the trip and performed their work from several temporary or inadequate locations before the convent was completed in 1752, making it the oldest surviving building in the Mississippi River Valley.

Ursuline is also the longest running all-girls school and the oldest Catholic school in America; it was also the first to teach slaves, Creoles, and Native Americans. For some years in the 1800s, it was the official residence of the city's archbishops and the unofficial home of vampires.

The story goes that a group of young girls were sent over from France to provide proper wives for the male French settlers. Upon arrival by ship, each with her entire belongings in a single coffin-shaped suitcase, they were housed at the Ursuline Convent. Collectively, they were called *filles à la cassette* ("girls with a cassette"), which was shortened to "casket girls." When some cases were found to be empty, hyper-imaginative residents thought the casket girls were smuggling vampires into New Orleans. Legend has it that the convent's third-story dormer windows are sealed with bolts blessed by the Pope in order to contain the undead in the attic.

The convent holds numerous points of interest. Right inside the front entrance is the original cypress staircase, carved from a single piece of wood, and a grandfather clock that the nuns brought with them from France in 1727. The main building is filled with dozens of oil paintings, religious statues, and bronze busts. Out back is a walled courtyard with life-sized statues of praying nuns, including Henriette Delille (see p. 174), a New Orleans Creole who founded the first-ever order comprising free women of color.

Address 1100 Chartres Street, New Orleans, LA 70116, +1 504.529.3040 | Hours
Mon–Sat 10am–4pm | Tip The chapel next door, at 1116 Chartres, has had a variety
of names. It was originally called Sainte Marie de l'Archeveche and later Holy Trinity,
then became St. Mary's Italian Church. In 1976, the name was changed for the last time
to Our Lady of Victory. Inside the church is the original Pilcher organ, built in 1890, and
an unusual stained-glass window that features Andrew Jackson.

107__Villalobos Rescue Center
Dogs with a cause

No one ever expected a dog shelter would become a popular attraction. But this is New Orleans, where the cemeteries are tourist destinations and folks will stand in line for an hour to get a small hunk of dough thrown into a deep fryer. Founder of Villalobos Rescue Center (Villalobos means "village of wolves") Tia Maria Torres opened her first shelter more than 20 years ago near Los Angeles. She paired abandoned pups, mostly the maligned and misunderstood pit bulls, with prison parolees who needed jobs and proved to be ideal caretakers. *Pit Bulls & Parolees*, a reality TV series about Torres' program on Animal Planet, ratcheted up the profile for Villalobos, landing Torres on programs like *The Daily Show with Jon Stewart* and attracting four times as many orphan dogs to her shelter.

After Hurricane Katrina, Torres moved Villalobos and the TV crews to New Orleans because she felt the area most needed her efforts. The New Orleans shelter is in a kind of sketchy neighborhood, right at the base of the bridge crossing over the Industrial Canal and into the Lower Ninth Ward. It's easy to spot, as it occupies a huge 50,000-square-foot warehouse with approximately 400 dogs on the premises at any given time. Her bills to run the center are over $40,000 a month, paid for mainly through donations (all tax deductible of course).

Villalobos has become a hidden gem for visitors in the know, offering informational tours during limited hours. Come and look, but keep in mind that this is a place of business and not just a reality-TV set. Autograph seekers or cell-phone paparazzi are not encouraged here (though respectfully taken photos are allowed). If you're looking to volunteer, Villalobos is often in need of "Nightwalkers." The zombie-sounding name simply involves going out with a group (never alone) to give special-needs dogs some much-needed exercise.

Address 525 N Claiborne Avenue, New Orleans, LA 70117, +1 504.948.4505, www.vrcpitbull.net | **Hours** Tue–Fri noon–3pm, Sat noon–2pm | **Tip** Mardi Gras is often misperceived as girls-gone-wild, frat-party debauchery. The fastest way to dispel the myth is to point to the Krewe of Barkus Parade, which comprises dogs dressed up according to the theme of the year padding alongside or riding on floats through the French Quarter. The Barkus Parade always occurs two Sundays before Fat Tuesday.

108___Whitney Plantation
America's first slave museum

The Whitney Plantation is the first and only museum in the United States focused on slavery. It was envisioned by a self-described "rich white boy." John Cummings amassed his fortune as a lawyer and real-estate magnate in New Orleans. He spent 15 years and more than $8 million to create a unique – some might say eccentric – museum for how he personally thought slavery should be presented. Because he used no outside funds, Cummings neither had to appease any board members nor make a single compromise.

The museum was created with unprecedented documentation, including detailed records of the slaves from the original 1721 plantation, listing them by name, complexion of skin, skill sets, and countries of origin, plus an eight-volume study of the grounds conducted by a previous owner, along with nearly 4000 oral histories of Louisiana slaves compiled by the WPA in the 1930s.

The grounds are centered upon the Big House, a Creole main building with 11 outbuildings including the original kitchen, believed to be the oldest detached kitchen in Louisiana (the kitchen was always designed away from the house in case of fire); a storage shed; an overseer's house; a mule barn; and a plantation store. Cummings also bought and reassembled 20 slave quarters on the premises.

Most moving are the sculpture exhibits. One is dedicated to the largest slave revolt in American history. In 1811, just a few miles from the Whitney Plantation, 125 or more slaves rebelled. They were quickly overpowered, with nearly 100 killed during the uprising or executed afterwards. As a warning to other slaves, many were decapitated, their heads placed on spikes. Cummings commissioned Woodrow Nash to make 60 ceramic heads, which are set atop stainless-steel rods.

While largely hailed, Cummings has had to defend the Whitney Plantation from some criticism. He has been quoted as saying, "It is disturbing. But you know what else? It happened."

Address 5099 Louisiana Highway 18, Wallace, LA 70049, +1 225.265.3300, www.whitneyplantation.com | **Hours** Wed–Mon 9:30am–4:30pm | **Tip** If you want a more sanitized tour of plantations, the Whitney is not far from Old Highway 18 in Vacherie, LA, where you'll find Oak Alley, the most-visited plantation on the planet and a location for more than 40 movies and Beyoncé videos; the Laura Plantation, with a rich history and run by four generations of women; or the recently opened for tours Evergreen Plantation, which served as Don Johnson's home in the movie *Django Unchained*.

109_ Yvonne LaFleur

Elegance without pretense

Shopping at Yvonne LaFleur's namesake store is not an excursion; it is an experience. LaFleur, who opened her shop in 1969, is a trained seamstress and milliner. She offers her own lines of apparel (casual and couture) and carefully handpicks the other items. From the moment you step into the 10,000-square-foot shop, your posture straightens and you're transported back to a time when refinement was standard. Hats are everywhere, from felt or fur cloches trimmed with feathers to wide-brimmed straw hats adorned with silk flowers.

LaFleur says that the modern Southern lady changes outfits multiple times during the day and has an "after-five wardrobe." All can be found on LaFleur's racks and shelves: casual wrap dresses, business suits, beaded evening bags, cashmere capes trimmed in fox, silk stockings, chiffon bodice dresses with jeweled belts and feather skirts, and various styles of gloves displayed in an antique case. From brunch to ball to bridal (there's a separate boutique in the back), nowhere else will you find dresses appropriate for "Mother of the Queen" or "the King's Wife." And if necessary, the store alters everything on-site for free.

Despite the abundance of elegance, there is not an ounce of pretense to be found. LaFleur's knowledgeable staff is not only trained in wardrobe design, but also keeps customers' favorite champagnes and wines on hand. Gentlemen can wait at the fully stocked 72-foot-long bar nestled between the scarves and the gift-wrapping station. All of LaFleur's wrapping is decorated in violets (as is her signature perfume). LaFleur says that violets represent loyalty, something she not only inspires in her customers (many are third generation) but also demonstrates herself. As fellow designer Coco Chanel once said, "A girl should be two things: classy and fabulous." She can achieve both at Yvonne LaFleur.

Address 8131 Hamson Street, New Orleans, LA 70118, +1 504.866.9666, www.yvonnelafleur.com | Hours Mon–Sat 10am–6pm (Thu open till 8pm) | Tip If you're looking for some shoes to match your latest Yvonne LaFleur ensemble, Feet First (4122 Magazine St) is a family-owned and operated store, and the city's largest independent shoe and accessories retailer.

110_ Zephyr Field
Field of dreams – and a pool

The New Orleans Zephyrs are a minor-league baseball team, the Triple-A affiliate of the Florida Marlins. The Zephyrs moved to New Orleans in 1993 but are a franchise that has existed for more than 100 years and played for five cities. The team holds the record for the most ever strikeouts (29) from a 24-inning game (also a record). In spite of the strikeouts, the Zephyrs beat the Nashville Sound 5 to 4 in that game. Their history includes stars Andre Dawson, Tim Raines, Graig Nettles, and Hall of Fame member Phil Rizzuto; the organization was also a managerial stepping-stone for Felipe Alou and Billy Martin.

Their stadium is on Airline Highway, which has quite the history itself, situated right next to the NFL Saints training facility, about 10 minutes from the airport. Airline Highway is famously identified with Governor Huey "the Kingfish" Long, who advocated and then built the state highway system as part of his campaign promise. His younger brother, Earl Long, was said to be the beneficiary when, as the new governor, he used the now fastest way to get from the state capitol building in Baton Rouge to his mistress in New Orleans, burlesque performer Blaze Starr, aka "Miss Spontaneous Combustion."

The stadium, nicknamed the "Shrine on Airline," was built in 1995 and is considered one of the best in minor-league baseball. There are 10,000 chair-backed seats with cup holders and 16 luxury suites. But what makes the ballpark a special and unique place to take in a game is an unusual feature in right field. There stands the Coors Light Party Shack, an outdoor bar that overlooks a swimming pool and two hot tubs. If you're lucky, you can catch a home run in one hand while holding a cold beer in the other, as you stand chest-deep in a swimming pool. In New Orleans in August, there is no better place to watch a baseball game than from inside the swimming pool in Zephyr Field's outfield.

Address 6000 Airline Drive, Metairie, LA 70003, +1 504.734.5155, www.milb.com | Tip
Near the ballpark is the New Orleans Saints training facility (5800 Airline Drive). During
the summer you can watch the Saints' practice sessions for free, unless it's so hot the team
chooses to take their workout indoors. In New Orleans in summer, it is often too hot. You'd
be advised to call ahead (+1 504.733.0255).

111__Zulu Social Aid & Pleasure Club

Cuckoo for coconuts

The story goes that in 1908, a small group of African-American laborers formed a club called the Tramps. Inspired by a variety-show skit featuring actors wearing grass skirts and dressed in blackface to parody Zulus, the Tramps changed their name and took to the streets in the next Mardi Gras parade dressed as a vaudeville version of African kings with lard cans for crowns and banana stalks as scepters. In 1916, they became an official Carnival krewe known as the Zulu Social Aid & Pleasure Club. Like all krewes, they took care of their members' needs and carried out other benevolent acts for the community.

The Zulu parades became most famous for their coconut throws. Unable to afford the expensive glass beads then used by other krewes (today cheap plastic beads are used instead), they painted and decorated coconuts, and started slinging what became a much-desired memento. In 1987, the Zulus were denied insurance coverage because of lawsuits from coconut-related injuries. The following year Governor Edwin Edwards signed into law the "Coconut Bill," removing liability from injuries resulting from tossed coconuts and enabling the tradition to resume.

In 1978, the organization opened a new home on North Broad Street. The building, painted in Zulu colors of yellow with black trim, holds their offices and a lounge for members and their guests. On the opposite side of Broad Street is the Zulu Memorabilia Shop. They sell inexpensive collectibles: beads, T-shirts, key chains, go-cups, plush toys, dress-up Afro wigs, straw skirts, and plastic Mr. Big Stuff cigars. There are more expensive one-of-a-kind objects like bobblehead dolls and ceramic and painted coconuts, plus the highest-priced item in the shop, the signed and numbered annual Zulu Social Aid & Pleasure Club poster.

Address Zulu Social Aid & Pleasure Club Memorabilia Shop, 807 N Broad Street, New Orleans, LA 70119, +1 504.827.1559, www.kreweofzulu.com | Hours Memorabilia shop: Mon–Sat 10am–6pm. Club: by member-invitation only | Tip The best time to visit the Memorabilia Shop is in January and February, when it's stocked up for Mardi Gras. Similar to the streetcars in New Orleans, which come when they come, the shop posts its hours as 10am to 6pm Monday through Saturday, but is instead open when they're open and closed when they're closed. Welcome to NOLA.

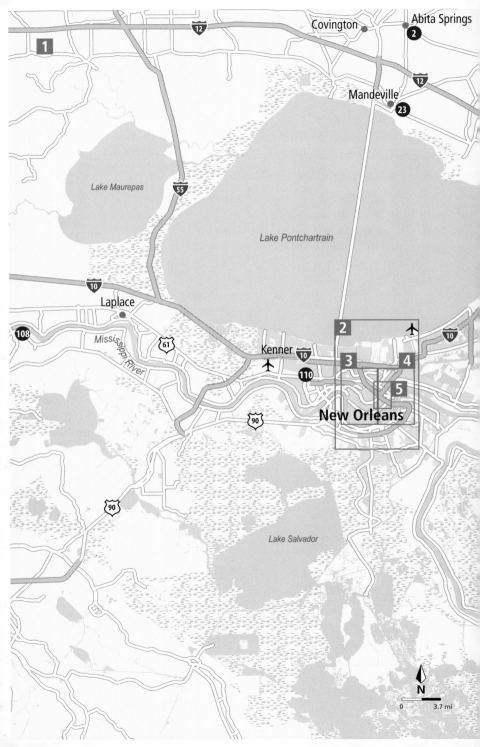

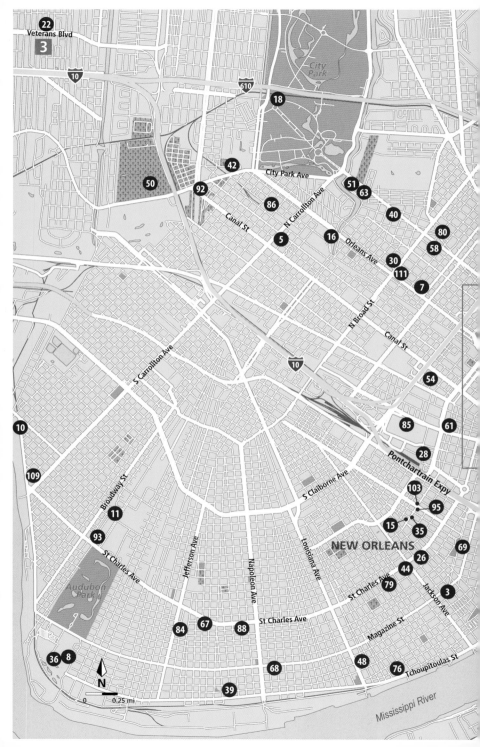

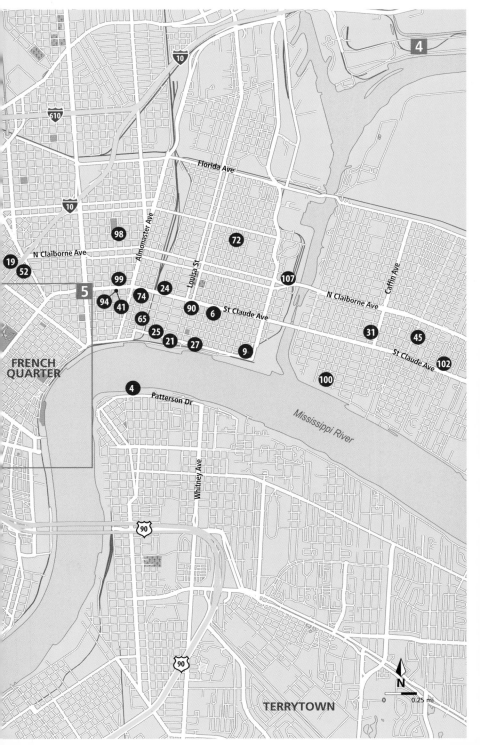